SIGNALS
FROM THE SOUL

SIGNALS
FROM THE SOUL

HOW OUR SOUL TELLS US WHAT WE NEED TO KNOW

ANN MULLER

Inner Self Press
Palm Springs, California

Inner Self Press
innerselfpress.com

© 2011 by Ann Muller

All rights reserved under International and Pan American copyright conventions. No part of this book may be reproduced or utilized in any form, by electronic, mechanical, or other means, without the prior written permission of the publisher, except for brief quotations embodied in literary articles or reviews.

Quotation in the introduction is from *Odyssey of the Soul: Apocatastasis* by Pamela Chilton and Hugh Harmon, © Pamela Chilton (Rancho Mirage, CA: Quick Books Publishing, 1997), p. 1.

Cover design by Jessica Stevens
www.design-savvy.com
Cover photo by Lauren Natalie Photography
www.laurennatalie.com

ISBN-10: 0983653208
EAN-13: 9780983653202
LCCN: 2011929936

Printed in the United States of America

10 9 8 7 6 5 4 3 2 1

To my brother, Thom, my rock
To Zach, my shining example of what can be accomplished

And to anyone who has ever asked,
"Why is this happening to me?"

Contents

Acknowledgments.. ix
Introduction xi
   1. Learning the Basics 1
   2. The Origin of Poor Eyesight 13
   3. Healing Poor Eyesight............................ 25
   4. Stuck in a Troubled Relationship 35
   5. The Origin of a Birth Defect...................... 45
   6. Adoption: Who Really Chooses Who?.............. 55
   7. The Perils of Ignoring Intuition................... 67
   8. The Soul Lessons of Sexual Abuse 77
   9. Healing Sexual Abuse............................ 87
  10. Washing It All Away 99
  11. Telling Mom................................... 109
  12. Healing My Other Ages of Abuse................ 117
  13. The Price of Unexpressed Emotions 127
  14. Don't Trade Me In.............................. 137
  15. Angels and Dreams 147
  16. Hidden Marriage Programs..................... 155

17. The Purpose of an Evil Life 165
18. How to Avoid Karma from an Evil Life 177

Reflections 187

Sample Neuro-Muscular Response Testing 193

Sample Hypnosis Inductions 201

How to Find a Regression Therapist 209

Light the Earth 211

Acknowledgments

My most heartfelt gratitude to the following people for their advice and support:

To Pamela Chilton, C.Ht., and Hugh Harmon, Ph.D., authors of *Odyssey of the Soul: Apocatastasis,* for writing the book that inspired me to take my own soul journey, and for all they have taught me along the way. Special thanks to Pamela, my mentor and my friend, for helping my inner levels to heal and for her steady guidance and help with this book.

To Carolyn Bond, my editor, for helping me develop my transcripts into a coherent book, and for teaching me to talk to my reader as if we're sitting at a kitchen table.

To Wendy J. Carrel, Author Ambassador, for embracing my message and helping me spread the word.

To Marilyn Parsons, fellow voyager, for her great energy and positive feedback from a very discerning reader.

To Dr. Gabriele Alpers, my soul sister, for her inspiring commitment to find the lessons in her childhood.

Introduction

What if we could look at our lives from a perspective where everything—large and small, good and bad—makes sense? What if we could understand the reasons for everything that happens in our day-to-day reality? We can. This is true for all of us and this is how I discovered it.

I thought all I wanted in life was to be happy. But even when I was happy, I always wanted more. My mother used to say, "Oh, Ann, you're never satisfied." And she was right. No matter how good things were, I always thought there had to be something more—more fun, more thrilling, more rewarding, more anything. Somewhere deep down I knew I was right. I just had to figure out where to look. Models were hard to find. Even my happiest friends were unhappy with something in their lives.

My dissatisfaction started when I was a small child. I grew up in the Midwest with conservative parents. They lived by the rules. I thought the rules were stupid. Who made up those rules anyway? I coped with my situation by living an imaginary life with imaginary friends where nobody had to be perfect and everyone was happy. By the time I was in college I had both feet planted in reality—but I did major in speech and drama. The fantasy world of the theater seemed a good compromise.

After college I continued in the theater as a stage manager, and later I started an online business that allowed me to travel the world. Even though my life was exciting, more often than not, no matter where I was or what I was doing, I was thinking about what might be next: maybe it would be even better. As I got older I began to wonder: what am I really looking for? Somewhere I read something about living a contented life. I looked up the definition of contentment—to be happy with one's lot. That's what I wanted! I didn't just want to be happy with what I was doing or how I was feeling; I wanted to be happy with everything in my life no matter what was happening. I started looking for the reasons why I wasn't content. First I sifted through my childhood and early relationships. Surely the answers had to be there. But that wasn't very productive. Then I tried talk therapy. That didn't help much either. So I went to a bookstore to see if someone else knew the answer.

I started with books about effective habits and releasing the tiger within. Then I moved on to books on thoughts and emotions and the law of attraction: Think it and it will come. Your thoughts create your reality. If you don't like your reality, just change your thoughts. If your emotional responses are causing problems, change them. You can even heal your body with affirmations—just repeat over and over the end result you are looking for. It must have worked for somebody. Those books were bestsellers. But none of them worked for me, no matter how hard I tried. I had small successes changing my thoughts, but my emotions didn't respond at all. And then there was the past. The past is past, they said. Just move on. Right. Easier said than done.

Somewhere along the line I learned about the subconscious mind. All our memories and the emotional programs created by our thoughts are located in the subconscious, and it's possible to go there and change them. That sounded promising. You can only access the subconscious in an altered state, so I found a hypnotherapist to help me. She had me explain to my subconscious why I no longer thought and felt the way I used to. The results were dramatic. But after a while the old thoughts and emotions returned and I was right back where I started. I figured that even though this method made so much sense in theory, something must still be missing.

While I was doing the hypnotherapy work, I started reading about the spiritual aspect of our lives. At first I was resistant to the word *spiritual* because I thought it meant religious dogma. But I learned it didn't mean that at all. We are spiritual beings living a human life. We're all connected because we all come from Spirit. There is a bigger picture. Go within and find your spiritual essence, the books said. Get quiet and meditate. Okay, but what about all those thoughts chattering away in my head? And what about this bigger picture—how does the muck of our day-to-day lives fit into it? And why would a spirit want to live a human life anyway when it could hang out in the peace and joy and love and light of the spirit realms? That seemed like the ultimate contentment to me.

The next leg of my journey was discovering past lives. I didn't believe in past lives, yet how could all those people in all those books heal illnesses and phobias and bad habits by going to their past lives if they didn't have any? As I read story after story I became curious why some people healed completely after a regression, others only partially, and some not at all. I also wondered why a soul needed to live so many lives. Some souls lived hundreds of them. This was definitely worth exploring.

By this time I knew a little bit about a lot of things. There was the human side of us—our everyday lives with our thoughts and emotions, bodies, relationships, our failures and our successes, our physical and emotional dysfunctions. Then there was the spiritual side—the soul entering a human body and then leaving it to return to Spirit, only to do it all over again. There was something called the Higher Self, although every book defined it differently. And there was white light and messages from Spirit and so many exciting things. But I still couldn't put it all together.

Then I found a book that connected the dots. While I was in Palm Springs to visit my brother, I made an appointment with a local psychic. I thought it would be fun to see what was ahead for me. On her coffee table was a book titled *Odyssey of the Soul, Book I: Apocatastasis*. I picked it up and read the dedication: "Dedicated to Spirit—For Those Who Seek The Answers To The Past, The Present, The Future." Wow! Maybe this would clear up everything. Then I turned to the first chapter, which began:

> There is a part of you that knows everything there is to know about you. It can tell you why you are in this world and where you were before you came here. It can state both Universal Truths and the Personal Truths you need to know to get where you want to go. It can talk about your future, your present, and your past. It can tell you about the people in your life—why you are involved with them, what you might want to learn from them, and what you have to teach them. It can help you become closer in your relationships or cut the ties that bind you to them. This part knows a great deal more about you than any psychic ever could. Further, it can heal you instantly, although it may take you longer to allow, or even hold onto the healing.
>
> This part of you is the you that always was and ever will be. It is your Higher Self.

I devoured the book. The authors were regression hypnotherapists who helped their clients heal their physical and emotional dysfunctions by finding the soul reasons for them. And there was a twist. What needed to be healed was a thought. At a certain moment in the past, a thought was formed in response to an experience that created an emotion that created an imbalance. The dysfunction was a signal from our soul, letting us know about the imbalance. The thought could have been formed during an event in this life or in a past life. But simply going to that past moment wasn't enough. You had to alter the thought.

This book offered exactly what I had been looking for. The role of thought was the missing link. I searched out the authors and found they lived in the next town! I called and made an appointment with one of them. This was my chance to learn how to fix everything in my life that was preventing me from being content. Maybe I could really push the envelope and find that elusive phenomenon called joy. So I began a series of hypnotherapy regression sessions that turned out to offer much more than I could ever have imagined.

All the things I thought were wrong with my life were actually signals from my soul that there was something I needed to learn. So I started addressing them one by one. I discovered I had shut down my emotions in the womb (chapter 6), and I learned the price of unexpressed emotions (chapter 13). My failure at marriage came from a thought at age eight (chapter 16), and I stopped remembering my dreams in seventh grade (chapter 15), also because of a thought. My poor eyesight had its source in a first-century life (chapter 2) and was triggered in this life at age eight (chapter 16). A congenital heart defect originated in an eighteenth-century life (chapter 5). My inability to leave a troubled marriage was from a third-century life (chapter 4). And I learned the soul reason why I was adopted (chapter 6) as I altered all the emotional programs the adoption caused.

These were all unlearned soul lessons. In each life there is a lesson that our soul sets out to learn. If we don't learn the lesson in that life, we have to try again in another. Before we're even born, the soul plans the major conditions of our life that create the opportunities and challenges to learn those lessons (chapter 6). These challenges often manifest as dysfunctions. Any emotional or physical dysfunction—a fall that leads to a life of pain, a difficult relationship, financial problems, illness or disease, a bad habit or addiction, to name a few—is a signal of an unlearned lesson. When we find the origin of the dysfunction and heal it by learning its lesson, we no longer need the signal.

This book tells my story, or rather the story of my soul and its odyssey through human lives. How did I find my soul's story? My soul told me.

"What," you may ask, "you talk with your soul?"

I do. You can too. And I highly recommend it because it changes your life profoundly. Our soul uses our mind to form thoughts that create the conditions in our lives to help us learn what we came to Earth to accomplish. So when we're feeling baffled and need guidance, we can ask our soul. It knows everything about us, and it tells us what we need to pay attention to. When we shift our perspective and see our lives from our soul's point of view, everything makes sense. And when everything makes sense, we can change what we want to change and create the life we want.

So how did this new perspective change my everyday reality? I almost hesitate to tell you because it sounds too good to be true. Let me put it this way: all my longtime friends are asking me, "What happened to you? You're so happy. Whatever you're doing, I want to do it."

I am happy. I'm finally content. I'm even living with joy. Why? Because everything makes sense now. Everything I thought was wrong with my life turned out to be part of my soul's plan to learn. Now when something happens that doesn't make sense, I know where to go to get answers. My soul can tell me.

The following eighteen chapters contain the transcripts of sessions with hypnotherapist Pamela Chilton, one of the authors of *Odyssey of the Soul*. In these sessions we tracked various physical and emotional dysfunctions to their originating thought and altered that thought. During this work I also learned to connect with the Higher Self part of my soul for guidance and protection.

The chapters of regressions are followed by afterthoughts concerning how this process has changed my life, and by an invitation for all of us to light the earth with our own light. Three appendices include a discussion and samples of the two methodologies used in the therapy sessions: hypnosis and Neuro-Muscular Response (NMR), and suggestions for how to find a competent regression hypnotherapist if and when you are ready for one.

What I came here to learn may be different from what you came here to learn, but the way to learn our lessons is the same for all of us. These transcripts illustrate step by step how to find unlearned lessons and what to do about them. Hopefully reading my stories will inspire you to find yours. It's the reason you're living your life.

CHAPTER 1

LEARNING THE BASICS

I finished the book, picked up the phone, and dialed. This was it! This was my chance to find out everything I'd ever wanted to know about myself and my life. I had so many unanswered questions.

I left a rambling message on the authors' voicemail saying that I wanted to do what the people whose stories were in the book had done. I wanted to know everything. Could I start today?

The answer was yes. So I started that afternoon on the greatest adventure of my life. The authors, Pamela Chilton and Dr. Hugh Harmon, worked just down the road in Palm Desert. When I arrived and opened the door, there stood Pamela, the woman who would guide me to many places and times in the past. I had no fear of hypnosis but even if I did, the sight of her would have quelled it. Her beautiful blue eyes, framed by a soft pageboy hairstyle, radiated kindness and acceptance. I knew right away I would be safe on this woman's watch.

She led me through double doors into her office. The room was bright and sunny with framed certificates lining the walls.

And then I saw The Chair, an overstuffed blue recliner, slightly worn on the armrests and headrest. I would have many adventures in that chair. It was comforting to know many others had sat in that chair too.

Pamela asked me to have a seat. Across from me, next to the double doors, hung a framed quotation:

> The Greatest Revolution Of Our Generation
> Is The Discovery That Human Beings,
> By Changing The Inner Attitudes Of Their Minds,
> Can Change The Outer Aspects Of Their Lives.
>
> – William James

It sounded good to me. I had lots of outer aspects that could use some changing. I pulled up the recliner lever and settled in, ready to go.

"So tell me about yourself," Pamela said as she sat down in a rolling chair next to me. "Why are you here?"

"Well, I just read your book and I want to know *everything*," I answered. "I want to find out about my past lives. I grew up Catholic so I never really believed in past lives. But I do now. And I want to know about my childhood. I don't remember anything before the age of six.

"I've had a good life," I continued. "The older I get and the more stories I hear of people's experiences, I'd have to say I've had it pretty easy. My parents loved me. Nobody beat me. I've been successful in my careers.

"But I was adopted, so I probably have some worthiness issues, and I was born with a weird heart and a missing toenail on my right foot. I'd love to find out about those now that I know congenital stuff often comes from a past life. My eyesight is pathetic, and I think I've been emotionally unavailable all my life. Those are my biggies. I just want to know about everything. Where do we start? How about finding a past life?"

"Well, Ann," Pamela explained, "before we get to that, the best use of today's consultation is to review some information about the mind and about our human purpose so you understand where we're going and what we're doing when you're in hypnosis. I'll hypnotize you next time, I promise.

"Because we're going to be working with the subconscious and Higher Self levels of your mind, and because everything you will learn is part of your spiritual quest, we need to be certain you understand the basics. It's like reading the whole recipe before you start to cook."

"Okay. Shoot."

"You know from the book that we are all spiritual beings living a human experience," she began, "and that the ultimate purpose of our human experience is to reconnect with that part of us that is our spirit, our true self.

"If you think of your spirit, or soul, as having vibration or energy frequencies, in order to embody, your spirit has to slow down its energy frequencies to be compatible with the energy frequencies of the physical body—which are much lower than those of spirit. The more you slow down your vibrational frequency, the less awareness and understanding you have. So your spirit doesn't want to slow down its whole self, nor could it; its vibration is really too big. So it slows down a portion of itself. That's the part that enters the body, and it's the part you think of as 'you.' But our spirit keeps the major part of itself in that higher frequency that it has attained over many lifetimes of learning, of gaining awareness and understanding. This we call the Higher Self. Are you with me so far?"

I nodded yes.

"Good. Now, when we talk about the mind, we are not talking about the brain. Many people think they are one and the same. They aren't. While you are embodied, your mind *uses* your brain to carry out the mental and physical functions of your body. When your body dies, the brain will die, but your spirit and your mind will not die. They will remain connected, and everything that has ever happened to you in this lifetime will still be there, recorded in your mind.

"There are three levels of the mind. The conscious mind is your everyday mind, so to speak. It steers the ship. The subconscious mind is like a vast storehouse of many parts. It's the storehouse of your beliefs and of your emotions and of your memories. It's the storehouse of nature's programming—it's where the cells of your body are programmed. It is also the transmitter and receiver of all spirit communication. The higher mind, or Higher Self, is the super consciousness part of your mind. It is the part of your mind that has stayed in the realm of spirit. If all three levels are not in agreement, you will be notified with a signal of physical and/or emotional dysfunction."

"Now, it's important to know that the Higher Self does not know all, or you wouldn't be here on Earth living your life. Your Higher Self is certainly aware of more than what you're aware of in the body, partly because you have blinders on, in a sense. These blinders are your emotions and your beliefs, and your programming and the ability to be programmed, and the part of you that will believe what someone else tells you whether it's true or not because you like the person, or they're in authority, or whatever.

"The Higher Self, that higher frequency, is free of all that. That's why it's our best guide through life. Some people call it the intuitive self, the over soul, the spiritual self, the Atman. I like to call it the Higher Self because it keeps it clear that it's the higher vibration of our own spirit. The part that's in the body is the lower vibration.

"Now, when the people in the book came in with disease or chronic pain, with a phobia, a habit they couldn't break, excessive anger, addiction, or something like that, you'll remember we always had to find the *origin* of the dysfunction. There was a beginning point for the dysfunction—an experience that first created the thoughts and beliefs to which the emotions became attached. Then something triggered it. How did we find it? We asked their subconscious mind."

"So are you saying," I asked, "that *everything* has an emotional origin? There's an emotional program that is causing it?"

"Most everything has an emotional origin, yes."

"If I get cancer there's an emotional program that's causing it? And it can come from this life or a past life?"

"Yes, although there can be physical contributing factors as well."

"What about if I trip on a sidewalk and stub my toe? I did that last week."

"That's a warning," Pamela explained. "You'll hear me say this more than once: *Everything* happens for a reason. *Nothing* is arbitrary. Stubbing your toe is a warning from your subconscious mind. Remember, the subconscious controls the body. And it uses the body to send you messages. The cancer is a message that there is an emotion that is causing imbalance. Stubbing your toe is a message to be careful, or don't trip yourself up, or watch where you're going. You're stumbling on your path. You need to look at what's going on in your life."

"So *everything* happens for a reason?" I asked. "*Everything*? Even something like a flat tire? Or what if I get a vitamin tablet stuck in my throat. That happened to me once."

"Yes, Ann. And we'll find out what those things meant at the time in your life that they happened. I'm writing them down now." Sure enough, she had a clipboard in her lap that I hadn't even noticed. It was turned sideways so she was writing on it horizontally.

"One other question before we go on," I asked. "If all we need to do to get rid of all the muck in our lives is go to the subconscious, why doesn't everyone just do that?"

"They don't know," was the answer. "Did *you* know before you read the book? Did *you* know that everything you do, think, and feel has a reason, a lesson in it? Only by understanding the mind can we truly understand the purpose of our human lives."

"So," I asked, "nothing 'just happens'? It seems a little daunting to have to find a reason for everything. But I guess finding reasons is better than constantly wondering 'Why is this happening to me?'"

"You're right," Pamela answered. "It is.

"Now, let's talk about programming a little bit," she continued. "We like to say we were programmed when we were a child, which is true. But the real truth is we program *ourselves* as a child because it's what we allow in, what we choose in that instant to believe, that forms the program. You spill the milk and your mother says, 'You're a clumsy oaf.' If, at that instant, we don't think, 'No I'm not, the milk was in the wrong place,' the subconscious says, 'Okay, we're a clumsy oaf.' Now our program has been built in and we still do it today. We're habitually clumsy.

"How do you change that program? As Albert Einstein said, we can't solve problems by using the same kind of thinking we used when we created them. So we must go to our subconscious and convince it of a new program. Now to get to the subconscious, we have to ask our conscious mind to take a step back. This is done in an altered state.

"Another term for altered state is hypnosis. Many people are afraid of hypnosis because they have misconceptions about it. Have you ever been driving in your car and all of a sudden arrived at your destination and had no recollection of the trip?"

"More often than I'd like to admit," I answered. "What was that? Where was I? And how did I manage to drive and not get into a wreck?"

"You were in a light hypnotic state. Your conscious mind stepped back. Your subconscious mind was driving the car. It knew where you were going and how to get there safely. Were you daydreaming about something?"

"Probably," I responded. "Or I was just zoned out."

"Zoning out, as you call it, is going into an altered state, into a light hypnosis. You *know* that had there been an emergency on the road you would have come right back to your conscious mind, right? Well, it's the same in hypnosis. If you were in that chair in hypnosis and someone yelled 'fire,' you'd be out of hypnosis in a minute. That's the misconception many people have. They think they lose control to the hypnotist. Not true. You are in complete control.

"People go to a hypnosis show, and there's this hypnotist on stage making people quack like a duck. You're thinking that those people would never quack like a duck if they knew what they were doing, so they are being controlled. But they're not. On an inner level they're agreeing to be part of a show. The hypnotist is very skilled at picking the kind of person out of the audience who will be willing to be part of the show, who will allow themselves to be suggestible. But if that hypnotist told one of them to kill somebody in the front row, they wouldn't do it because it's against their moral programming. They would snap right out of hypnosis."

"I'm not afraid of hypnosis," I said in an effort to speed things up. "So let's go. Is there anything else I need to know beforehand?"

"Well, Ann, you have a very quick mind, very fast, all over the place. To hypnotize someone like you, it's necessary to take time relaxing the body and talking to the body, because the subconscious is in control of the body. If you begin hypnosis by talking about the body so that the person is focusing their mind on the body, you're already talking to the subconscious.

"When you focus on your scalp, for example, and think to yourself, 'relax,' you're talking to your subconscious. You're starting to pull in its attention. 'I'm thinking of the scalp. Relax it. I'm thinking of my eyelids. Relax the eyelids.' You're narrowing the attention and focus of the subconscious so by the time you're ready to do whatever you're going to do in hypnosis, you're in that lock-in with the subconscious, you have eliminated all those distracting thoughts."

"How is hypnotherapy different from hypnosis?" I wanted to know.

"Hypnosis is getting a message to the subconscious mind," Pamela explained. "But if the subconscious blocks that message, then therapy is needed to release the block or alter the old program. Ideally, as we grow in age, previous ages—our inner ages—are content. Your three-year-old self became a part of the past. But if the lesson wasn't learned and that three-year-old feels incomplete or distressed, she does not move into the past. Then you have an active inner child—or sometimes a past life personality. So you need to reprogram that age or personality.

"Say you want to program, 'You can trust people you love.' If there is a block, if an inner resistance from a past program has been triggered, then the new program won't last. You have to remove the block with therapy with that inner child or past life personality."

"So that's why sometimes The Secret doesn't work. Right?"

"Right," Pamela answered.

"In the book you did some kind of muscle testing," I said. "I think it's called NMR. You used it to find origins and causes of dysfunctions. It seemed to be a real time-saver."

"Yes," Pamela replied. "Have you ever heard of applied kinesiology?"

"Yeah. A chiropractor used it once to check tablet dosage," I said.

"There are very specific criteria that are important to getting accurate results with muscle response. Dr. Harmon and

I have developed a protocol to meet these criteria called Neuro-Muscular Response, or NMR for short.

"I'm going to demonstrate the steps important to getting accurate results. Many people feel once they have experienced NMR they can do it with others. I want to show you why that isn't a good idea. It is a very, very valuable tool, but like a surgeon's scalpel, it can do great harm in the wrong hands."

Pamela demonstrated NMR using my legs, not my arm as my chiropractor had. She said it didn't matter which muscle of the body is used, but the large muscle that controls the leg does not tire easily. She gave me a statement to repeat. She had one hand on each ankle. After I made the statement she would say 'hold,' and I would try to resist her pulling my ankles together. If the answer to the statement was yes, my legs stayed strong. If the answer was no, my legs weakened and my ankles came together no matter how hard I resisted.

She explained that using statements instead of questions elicits more definitive responses, and how those statements are prefaced affects the response. Prefacing a statement with 'my cells' or 'my body,' for example, directs the subconscious to respond for the cells or the body. Prefacing a statement with 'my Higher Self' directs the subconscious to respond for the spiritual level of the soul. When the statement has no preface, the subconscious mind itself responds with its knowledge or programmed beliefs. Knowledge and programmed beliefs are significantly different, as I was to discover over the course of my work with Pamela.

Then Pamela demonstrated how NMR can be misused. She asked me to state my name but to make it a false name and think to myself: that is not my name. My muscle response was strong, indicating the statement I made was true.

"But it's not true," I protested.

"What isn't true? The false name you spoke aloud or the thought that it is not your real name? That's the problem with all muscle testing. If you think something different from what you say aloud, the response is to what you are thinking, not what you are saying. The person being tested has to keep his or her thoughts focused on the statements they make. Otherwise the testing is useless at best and dangerous at its worst."

Pamela also showed me how the therapist's thoughts can affect the testing. She had me state my true name, but the muscle went weak. "I did that," she said. "I was thinking 'no, no, no,' which confused your subconscious just enough to weaken the leg muscle, giving us a false response. I wanted you to see how the practitioner can and will influence the response by what he or she is thinking. Even the expectation of what an answer will be by either person can skew the results."

"Then why use it?" I asked. "How can anyone trust the answers they get?"

"You don't throw out valuable tools just because they can be misused," she responded. "You learn how to use them skillfully. It's true you would not want to have anyone use any kind of muscle testing on you who is not well trained or who has something to gain from it. Twenty years of doing this has taught me to pay attention to the NMR protocol, including the importance of how to word a statement. I would say I am successful in this 95 percent of the time. I always test important matters more than once to add to the accuracy of the testing.

"Now comes the hard part," Pamela said with a sigh. "What do you think about spirits?"

"Well, I watch *Ghost Whisperer*," I replied. "I think some move into the light but some hang around if they are troubled about something."

Pamela nodded. "Most people like to think everyone moves on when they die and that they become more enlightened. This is not true of everyone. When they don't move on into a more enlightened level, when they stay in the Earth planes, they keep the same mindset they had when embodied. They have the same beliefs, thoughts, and emotions, all of which can affect muscle testing responses considerably when they are attached to or around a person being tested. This is why we always begin NMR by testing for such presences."

Pamela and I tested to see if any spirits were with me, and there were none. We would do this at the start of every session.

By the end of this first session I was saturated with new information and eager to do a regression. I wanted to tackle my poor eyesight first. My eyes had been unusually dry and blurry the past few days; maybe my subconscious was suggesting my eyesight as a good place to start. We did some additional NMR and found that the origin of my poor eyesight was a thought in a past life.

"Can I come back tomorrow and explore this further?" I asked.

"We'll do that," Pamela answered, "but tomorrow I want you to simply experience hypnosis to see how you respond. We won't do any therapy."

I was disappointed, but I figured she knew best. I knew this was going to be different from my other hypnosis experiences. I was in the hands of a skilled, experienced hypnotist who understood not only the mind but the role of the mind in our soul's journey. She understood how it all fit together.

I scheduled a session with Pamela for the next day. That evening, of all that I had learned that day, what I thought about the most was that everything—large and small, good and bad— happens for a reason. There was so much about myself and my life I wanted to understand. Little did I know that I would soon learn things about myself I wasn't even aware of. My subconscious and my Higher Self would bring them all to my attention.

The next day Pamela led me through a hypnosis induction. First she helped me relax my body and my mind, and then she guided me to different levels of hypnosis. We established the finger responses my subconscious would use during hypnosis for "yes" (raising my right index finger) and "no" (raising my left index finger). Then she brought me back to my conscious level of awareness. Now I was ready for my first working regression.

Chapter 2

THE ORIGIN OF POOR EYESIGHT

Anyone who wears glasses knows poor eyesight has to do with the curvature of their eyes. But why did the curvature change? An optometrist can explain the physical reason, but what about the non-physical reason? In my first hypnotic regression I find, in a life lived long, long ago, the thought that is the origin of my poor eyesight in this life.

"Okay, Pamela," I said as I settled into The Chair, "let's find out about my eyesight. Anything more than six feet away has been a blur since I was eight years old. And I had to stop wearing my contact lenses a few years ago when my eyes got too dry, so now I'm back to glasses."

Pamela and I began the session by muscle testing with NMR for almost half an hour. (The transcript of this NMR session is the sample NMR session at the back of the book.) As before, she gave me a statement to make and I repeated it. Sometimes she had me say the same thing in different ways to see if the answer remained the same. Then we checked the answers with my Higher Self.

At the end of the previous session we had learned that my poor vision originated in a thought in a past life. Today the muscle testing revealed the reasons in this life: an emotional contributing cause was anger at age eight, and a physical contributing cause was the fact that my eyes were too dry.

I asked if finding and healing the originating thought would take care of everything or if I would have to continue to address the physical cause with eye drops and eye exercises. Pamela answered that sometimes healing the origin is enough, but sometimes the dysfunction also needs attention on the physical level.

Using NMR, we asked my Higher Self if I should work with the originating thought first. The answer was yes. I would work with my eight-year-old's anger later (for that regression, see chapter 16). To determine the lifetime of the origin we tested backward from today. It turned out to be a lifetime in the first half of the first century CE as a male living in Judea. I was an Essene, a cousin of Joseph and a second cousin of Jesus.

I had never heard of the Essenes. Pamela explained that Jesus was born into the tribe of the Essenes. They were a disciplined religious sect devoted to spiritual knowledge and teaching, and they gave special attention and instruction to children who showed signs of higher levels of consciousness.

With NMR we found the specific thought that was the origin of my bad eyesight: I didn't want to see. I had been present at the Crucifixion and didn't want to see what I was witnessing. Further NMR indicated that this was enough information to proceed with the regression and that my subconscious knew where to begin.

"As we do the past life," Pamela explained, "what will likely happen is that as I'm saying you're going back into time and I say you're there, at some point you're probably going to think, 'I'm very aware I'm in the chair and she's talking to me. I haven't lost my sense of here and now, but I am starting to get impressions or thoughts, or visuals or feelings of that life.'

"At that moment, if you decide to go with the thoughts, the feelings, the impressions, they will draw you more and more into that life, although you are unlikely to lose all your awareness of here. But if at that moment you become frustrated and think, 'No, no, I'm here in this chair,' you're going to start shutting off the impressions.

"So at that moment I forewarned you about, just relax and allow the impressions to come. And when impressions or visions or thoughts or feelings come into your mind, simply state them. If you try to figure them out during the regression, you're going to bring in too much of your analytical mind. You have your tape recording and you have your memory. You can figure out later what things meant. And because we have the NMR, it allows you to relax much more in the experience, to say what comes to your mind, and we can test where that came from later, which really frees you to just go with what's happening."

And so I was off to the first century in my first regression. Relaxing was going to be a challenge. I had to focus. (For the transcript of this induction, see the sample inductions at the back of the book.)

Pamela began, using her soothing hypnosis voice, so soft and gentle, breathy, like a mother urging her baby to sleep, "So as you relax in the chair, relax the jaws, relax the neck, relax the shoulders. That's it."

She kept going right down to my toes and then started counting backwards from 100. By 96, the numbers had faded away and I was drifting back through time century by century.

Pamela continued, ". . . back into that first half of the first century, into the body, into the being that you are in the first century, . . . shifting into that awareness. Becoming aware of yourself there in the time of the first century in the body that you have now in that first century, into the awareness, into the sense of knowing of self in that first century as the Essene. Taking a moment to become aware of your bearings, becoming very aware of your feet.... As you hear the sound of your own voice it anchors you more and more firmly into this time and place as I ask you, 'Your feet—are your feet covered or bare?'"

"Bare," my Essene answered. The voice was deep and sounded a little distant.

"And are you standing, sitting, or lying down?" Pamela asked.

"Standing."

"Are you standing indoors or outdoors?"

"Outdoors."

"Where you are standing, is the place familiar or unfamiliar to you?"

"Familiar."

"Describe your surroundings."

"I'm at the marketplace."

"Is it daylight or night?"

"Daylight."

"Are you alone or are there others?"

"There are many people."

"What are you doing?"

"Talking to someone."

"Look at the person you are talking to, and as you do, feel your *own body*, your *own* being. Now tell me—clothing, what are you wearing?"

"A long robe."

"Is the person you are talking to a man or a woman?"

"It's a man. As I talk to him I also keep an eye on what is going on around me."

"This man, is he young or old or in between?"

"In between. Middle-aged."

"How is he dressed?"

"The same as I am."

"And is this a familiar person to you?"

"Yes."

"What are the two of you doing here, in this place?"

"Just passing by each other. We are just acknowledging each other."

"What are the others doing?"

"Daily shopping and conversation."

"What is the exchange between you and this man?"

"Nothing intense. Just pleasantries."

"So all things seem rather quiet or pleasant today?"

"Yes."

"Good. Now think to yourself that you wish to go to an important event, to the next important event in your life. Be there now at three, at two, at one, and as you open your eyes, where do you find yourself?"

"My brother's house."

"Is your brother there?"

"Yes."

"Your brother's house, describe it."

"Stone, dark on the inside, like everybody else's house. Earthen vessels around."

"What's occurring here at your brother's house?"

"There's a baby, a baby boy. It's my cousin. Everyone is excited. There is something special about this baby. But there's something disturbing. There's lots of joy about this new little baby, but there's also like a cloud over him."

"What are your impressions of this baby boy?"

"I fear for it."

"Examine your feelings. What is your knowing?"

"Something is going to happen to this baby."

"Do you say anything to the family?"

"They know. Everybody knows. No, I don't say anything."

"Are the mother and father there?"

"Yes."

"Do you converse with them?"

"Just to say it's a beautiful baby."

"Is there more to know about this moment?"

"No."

"Then close your eyes again and think to yourself that you are going to the next important event in your life. You feel yourself being drawn there at three, to the next important event at two, and at one you open your eyes. What are you aware of?"

"The baby is grown up and he's talking to a crowd."

"Are you in the crowd?"

"I'm off to the side. He's my cousin and I'm there with the family. He's talking to this crowd. He's a teacher."

"What do you think of his teachings?"

"What he is saying is important, but it's going to get him in a lot of trouble."

"You're a teacher, too, right?"

"Yes."

"What do you teach?"

"Science, math, astronomy, that kind of thing."

"Have you taught your cousin?"

"Yes, but he's teaching spiritual things. He didn't learn this from me. This is a different kind of knowledge. He inspires people. And he teaches people about things not concrete. I teach concrete things. Jesus is his name, and he teaches about spiritual things."

"What do you think about these non-concrete things he teaches?"

"I think it's inspiring. And I think it's wonderful. But it's going to get him in trouble."

"Are you basing this on intuition or on what you observe?"

"Well, by now it's both. I've always worried about him ever since he was a baby. But now, politically—something is going to happen to him."

"Is the whole family of this mind, that something will happen?"

"Yes, everybody knows, but we don't want to stop him because it's *so* important what he's saying. He's helping so many people. He's helping so many people find peace. Their lives are so miserable, and he shows them that there's more than just physical reality."

"Does he still live with his family?"

"He's all over the place."

"Does he have followers?"

"Oh, yes. It's a movement. It's getting bigger and bigger."

"Does his family support him? Do you support him?"

"Oh, yes. But there's a *lot* of political repression. Everything is tightly controlled. He's really going against the grain and something is going to happen to him."

"Do you try to speak to him about this?"

"He knows. He's got to do it anyway. He's inspired. He's getting this from higher powers, and it doesn't really matter to him what's going to happen to him."

"Does it matter to you?"

"Yes. I don't quite understand why he doesn't care. I know how he *talks* about death and moving on. And it seems whenever it happens it's fine with him. I don't quite get that. I don't want to see him—it's not so much that I mind seeing him die. I don't want to see him tortured. That's my concern, that I'm going to see him be tortured. They don't just kill you, the Romans. They torture and make it painful."

"The young men in your tribe and the young women—are you taught how to withstand torture?"

"Yes, but it remains a real fear for me. So I stay on the sidelines. I know just being family I'm at risk also. But I still support him. I want him to do what he is doing. It's very important."

"Are you married yourself?"

"I don't have a family, no."

"Go now, close your eyes and see if your fears come to pass. Go to when that ominous feeling meets its manifestation.

Be there now at three, two, and one. Open your eyes and tell me what you see."

"I'm on a path on a hill. *Everyone* is there. I mean *everyone*. They've come from *everywhere*. They're going to crucify Jesus! And they're making him drag this *incredibly* heavy cross up this hill. And everybody wants to get to the front to see him. I can't cope. I'm back in the crowd. I don't want to see him. I don't want to look. He's not here yet. He's on his way. I hear they've stuck these thorns in his head."

"Do you know this? Were you told this?"

"I've heard from people who've seen him further down the hill that he's bleeding and it's just awful. But there's something about him, even though he's in pain and he's bleeding, and all those *physical* things, he seems to be out of body. But we all just see the physical pain that he's going through. I don't think I want to see it when he comes up the hill. I want to remember him in his beauty, talking to the crowds and seeing the inspiration on their faces as he talks."

"And as he comes up the hill, what do you do?"

"I take a quick peek and turn away."

"And what do you see in your quick peek?"

"Everything I've been told. He's dragging this incredibly heavy cross. The cross is on my side so I don't know if he's got thorns in his head or not."

"As you turn away, what do you look at?"

"The mountains in the distance."

"And what do you hear as you watch the mountains in the distance?"

"I hear the people around me. They're crying and moaning. Not hysterical, but just *so sad*. Very *sad*."

"And you are feeling...."

"Very sad. And angry—that the Romans can *do* this, that they have the kind of power that they can *do* this. And there's *nothing* we can do about it except find comfort in the community of my tribe. We stick together. But one false move, and they just come and drag you out of your house. We are *totally* controlled."

"How long are you here on the hill?"

"It seems like *forever*. And *then*, they get him to the top and they strap him to this cross."

"Do you see it or hear it?"

"I can't watch it. I hear it. I mean, I hear the noises of it and I hear the noises of the crowd. But I can't watch it."

"What happens next?"

"They leave him there. I take a look, one quick look before I go. I say a prayer that he can just go quickly and not suffer. Actually, I thank him for all his teachings, and for being so brave and doing it anyway and fulfilling his purpose. We all knew it was going to come to some kind of end like this, but he just did it anyway. And I tell him how brave I think he is and how sorry I am that these horrible, horrible people did this to him."

"When you turn away from him, where do you go?"

"I start walking down the hill. It's amazing how many people are staying there, watching him up there. But I just can't do it. Maybe it's because I knew him from when he was so little and because he is part of the family. But I don't want to see him up there. I don't want to look at him up there. I just want to remember him in his passion."

"Where do you go?"

"I start walking down the hill. I'm alone. I don't know where I'll go. I don't want to go home. It's so solitary. I'll probably go back to the meeting place in town."

"We will talk again," Pamela says. "Go to where you can find solace and peace, for we have more to discuss when we shall meet again. Allow yourself to rest. Rest your eyes from what you have seen. Rest your body. Rest your mind, rest your spirit, rest your heart. And as you allow yourself to rest,

[I let out a deep sigh and visibly relax] that's it—and shifting now your awareness back into this century, into the twenty-first century and into this wonderful body.

"Take a nice deep breath [I take a very deep breath], that's it—and think to yourself that this went very well, thanking the subconscious for its guidance and reminding it, now you, that the next time the regression occurs it will happen easily and comfortably as you go *deep* into that time and place. As you think of the lifetime that was spent then, send it light, thankful for a life well lived and for knowledge well gathered.

"And as you are relaxing, think of that inspiration seen on people's faces, that light. And as you think of that light that you saw, feel its presence there with your eyes, that *healing* energy you saw—so alive, so active, so present—is present now with you, present now in *your* eyes, in *your* sight.

"As you take the next deep breath, you merge easily and comfortably—body, mind, and soul—in that *perfect* alignment for your being today as Ann. With your next deep breath you find yourself very much here in this time and place. At one, at two, eager to do a little bit of testing and talking here, with you and me. At three, feeling that energy of you today, that *wonderful* healing energy that is *your* life force, that is *your* spirit. At four, coming up more and more now. And at five, stretching here at five, and giving me your impressions as you open the eyes."

After the regression I had many questions. For one thing, the experience of the regression had been very visual, yet I hadn't felt like I *was* the Essene man. I felt more like I was watching him. Pamela explained that like anything else, people become more comfortable with hypnosis as they do more of it. Many people start by feeling a bit of distance from the inner personality. Even after some experience with hypnosis, they may still feel more connection to some inner personalities while others will feel very foreign.

Another question was: How could I know that I hadn't made it all up? I already knew a lot about the Crucifixion from being raised as a Catholic. Pamela and I tested many details from the regression with NMR, which confirmed that I hadn't made any of it up. My conscious mind had interfered slightly, trying to make sense of the experience by analyzing it, but it had not interfered with what was happening or what I saw.

I had found the originating thought of my bad eyesight. My Essene had said several times he didn't want to look, he didn't want to see the Crucifixion. That thought had become imprinted in my subconscious. I had also learned a big lesson about the price of not looking at reality—which I had done a lot of in this life. If I didn't want to deal with something, I just wouldn't look, figuring that if I didn't see it, I wouldn't have to deal with it. But I now knew there is something to learn in everything that happens.

Chapter 3
HEALING POOR EYESIGHT

Okay, I had found the originating thought causing my poor eyesight. Now what do I do about it? In this session we return to my Essene and help him identify and learn the lesson of his lifetime. Then I am able to reprogram the subconscious thought "I don't want to see," using the screen of my mind located in my subconscious command center.

During the induction for this regression I establish the visuals for the center: a large room filled with office furniture with a freestanding blackboard on which I will write the old thoughts, erase them, and replace them with the new thoughts. After the regression, I check with NMR to make sure my subconscious has accepted the new thought.

We got right to it. Pamela cued up the tape to record the session and put on another tape of sounds of the waters of a lake washing up on shore, complete with chirping birds. After guiding me to relax my body from head to toe, Pamela continued, ". . . In this deep, deep relaxation, so similar to that deep, deep relaxation of sleep, the body moves itself into perfect balance, every bone rotating into its perfect position for balance, for walking, for standing, for sitting, for lying down. Within your skeletal system, those cells of your bones, every cell has a prime, optimum, perfect form. And within every cell is the memory, the realization of that perfect pattern, for its form and function. When you sleep, when you relax deeply, that pattern is what the cell uses to repair itself.

"Now, subconscious, is the conscious mind sufficiently relaxed at this time? [My "yes" finger lifts.] Good. Then moving deeper into the levels of hypnosis, so comfortably, so easily, drifting back through the centuries to the man that you were in the first half of the first century, in his place of rest and peace, as he hears my voice calling him forward.

"Standing on a hill, the hill on which so much is unfolding, so much to see, so much to think, so much to feel. Standing there, and Jesus has been placed upon the cross, a gruesome practice of the Romans. Are you there?"

"Yes."

"What do you see?"

"I'm in the crowds. I'm thinking that I never really listened with the intent to truly understand the message. I was more magnetized by the way he was able to mesmerize a crowd and the looks of hope on their faces and I never really listened to *him*. But now seeing him die this way, I'm going to think more about what he said and be a little less rigid about science and think more about spiritual things—because he died for that. And he was so unperturbed about dying—there's *something* there. There's something I have to think about."

"Very good."

"And I'm sorry I didn't do it while he was alive. I missed that opportunity. But it's never too late and I'm going to embark on finding out more about what he said and understanding it."

"Then are you saying that your thinking is that his death—his manner of death, his dying early—serves a purpose?" Pamela asked.

"Yes. I was watching him walk up that hill and watching it all happen, and I was *so* angry. And I couldn't look. I didn't want to see. I still don't want to look at him up there on the cross. I'm just going to walk back down to the marketplace. But I'm thinking, hmm, there was a reason for this. This is bigger than just him up there on that cross."

"So go down, now, to the marketplace. What frame of mind are you in?"

"I'm less angry. I'm more contemplative. I feel calm, a kind of peace. I don't know *why* or *how* or what it is exactly, but the anger is gone. There are others here, and they are feeling the way I'm feeling. It's a *calmness*. Once we're past the initial anger and outrage, there's a calmness and a peacefulness. We're almost in a daze."

"How do you account for this?"

"I don't know. It's like he's sending it to us."

"Are these people part of your own people, your own tribe, or are they a mixture of people?"

"A mixture. They are people he impacted."

"Are any of his apostles here?"

"No, they're not around."

"Any of his family other than yourself?"

"No."

"You can close your eyes on this scene and go to a time after this moment in which there are important events unfolding in your life, matters of importance for you. That's it. Be there now at three, two, and one. Where are you now?"

"I find myself gravitating more toward his followers—and not as a cousin but just as someone who wants to learn from him."

"Is there anyone in particular you go to?" Pamela asks.

"No, I go to groups because they're everywhere and they're tending to stick together. It's easy to find them and you can just walk into a conversation. They're very accepting, very generous. They'll invite anyone into a conversation. It's fascinating. They're talking about the soul and the kingdom of God within us and looking beyond this physical reality.

"It's an uplifting concept, a way to think about things. It really does make you feel you're not the end-all and be-all of the universe. But it's a positive feeling. I understand the message now. I'm thinking in broader terms rather than minutiae. It's definitely had an impact on me. And I have new friends. It's just broadened my horizons."

"Do you still associate with your family?"

"Oh, absolutely. And there's a tight bond there just from losing a family member."

"And Jesus's mother and father—are you still in connection with them?"

"They seem to understand the importance of his dying. There are moments when the anger comes, especially when you see the Romans on the street or you hear someone else being arrested and condemned to death. That brings up the anger. But other than those times, it's just an incredible peace."

"Okay. Close your eyes once more," Pamela instructs. "Are there any rumors about Jesus or any stories about him? What happened to his body after the cross?"

"I don't know if it's rumor or not, but they say his burial place is empty."

"Does the family talk about this among themselves?"

"I don't know."

"Do his disciples talk about it?"

"Of course."

"Okay. Close your eyes a moment. I wish you to move forward to the time of your death. Be there in the time and the circumstances and events surrounding your death, being aware *just* before your spirit leaves the body. That's it. Now, tell me, are you alone or are there others with you?"

"There are people around me. I'm on a bed. I'm just old."

"So your body is old. Weak, I assume?"

"Yes."

"The people around you, who are they?"

"There are a few from Mary's family, a few from mine and Joseph's family. It's very nice. Everyone's gathered around because I've been getting weaker and weaker. I think it is just time to go. They've come to say good-bye."

"So your life, up until this moment, what would you say occurred in your life after the death of Jesus? Did you continue to teach?"

"Yes. But I started to teach in a different way. I started to teach more to people who weren't in a position to become educated. I simplified things so that people who hadn't had education before could understand.

"I would take things I used to teach to the educated and mix them with the teachings of Jesus and integrate them and make them understandable. I started teaching everybody—the people who wouldn't have the chance to have that kind of education."

"Very nice. Now go to the moment of death when your spirit leaves the body. Tell me your thoughts as you leave the body."

"I see myself looking down on everyone standing there. I know I was ready to leave, and I know that I'm going to see Jesus or connect with Jesus's spirit. Actually, I'm pretty excited because I really think he'll be proud of me for the changes I made in my life and what I was able to accomplish with people. So it's very exciting for me."

"Follow that excitement and see where it takes you."

"Well, it takes me to this whiteness—and Jesus's spirit is right there! And he's so happy that I'm there and so complimentary to me and so proud of me. It's everything I expected it to be."

"Good. And as you look back over your life, ask that part of your spirit that knows: what did you learn and gain in this life?"

"Oh, the biggest lesson was that there's more to life than just the everyday human conscious reality. And the trick to a successful life is to get out of that and embrace the non-physical part of our lives, the part of ourselves that is spirit."

"Good."

"Not really successful—to be happy, to be joyous. And I did get pleasure and some joy, I think, out of the changes I made in my life. I never felt I truly experienced joy, but I definitely felt joyful about what I was doing."

"Now that you are here in this place of light, what are you feeling?"

"Oh, totally free!"

"Does that feel joyful?"

"Oh, absolutely! Very!"

"How would one find that back there on the Earth planes?"

"More spiritual work. Yes, I got more spiritual, but there were others *much* more spiritual than I was."

"Now," Pamela instructed, "allow yourself to go back into the lifetime you just left. You're being pulled right there, right now at three, right back to the hill. At two right back to where Jesus is on the cross in front of you. At one, I will say to you: If you will look into his face, you will discover something you lost, something you didn't gain. Are you prepared to do that?"

"Yes."

"What do you see?"

"Pure love. And peace. He's very peaceful and content."

"Okay. He lifts his head and looks at you. And do you see that pure love?"

"Oh yes."

"And here he is, in a place of suffering, yet . . . and yet what?"

"Even in a place of suffering, *love* is the ultimate. Love conquers all."

"So in your mind, as he looks at you from there on the cross, ask him, 'Do you suffer?' And what do you receive?"

"He says, 'Only my physical body suffers; my spirit does not suffer.'"

"Ask him, 'Can you stop your physical body from suffering?' What does he say?"

"He says, 'It's not suffering now. I let my body suffer up the hill to make a point. But it's not suffering now.'"

"Is this a surprise?"

"Oh yes. I couldn't even look at him."

"And now?"

"Now I could look at him until they take him down."

"And with that realization, you find yourself back up in that place you described as whiteness, that place where you see all that love, where you feel that joy. And as you look back now over your lifetime, tell me if there is anything you are shown or told is undone, not yet finished."

"Yes. That I can go further in connecting with all my levels of being. And I want to do that. Because what I did manage to accomplish was pretty good. [He laughs.] So that's fine with me!"

"Very good," Pamela said. "Then, as you move into your own joy, into your own bliss, into your own love, allow yourself, Ann, to feel that experience of that part of your spirit, to feel that vibration, that joy, that love, to know this is what guides you. This is what you reach for. For this is what you can, indeed, attain in this life.

"And now shine that whiteness, that light, on your eyes in this life. Focus now into your physical being in this century, looking deep into your own eyes. And as you look deep into your own eyes, you are receiving enlightenment about your eyes. You are being told what is important to know about your eyes so that the eyes see clearly. Ask your eyes, 'What do you need?'"

"Eyes, what do you need?" I ask.

"We need you not to be afraid to look," my eyes responded, "because if you look you will see, and if you see you will understand and you will gain knowledge. And knowledge is everything."

"Ask your eyes what they need to keep them moist."

"Eyes, what do you need to remain moist?"

"Love and joy," my eyes answered.

"Good. Then at this moment, see on the screen of your mind the words 'I was blinded.' And after that write: 'Once I was blinded, but now I see clearly.' Write: 'Every day my vision improves. Every day my eyes strengthen and move into the form, into the shape necessary for clear vision.' Write: 'My vision becomes clear daily.' Write: 'Every day my eyes become more and more perfect as they move towards perfect vision.'

"And write and think to yourself: 'I look for the joy in the suffering of others. I look for the joy in the tragedies of life. For I know in every event, good and bad, there are spiritual treasures unfolding. If people would but look for them, they would find them. If they would open their eyes and see clearly, they would know. Here is an opportunity to find the richness behind the seeming misfortune. The change has been thrust upon me.'

"Within every soul there is that knowing," Pamela continues, "but they forget. They turn away. They are fearful to see the suffering. They are fearful to see what they don't want to see. But you know that within them there is the part that is urging them to look, to behold, and to see: 'I bring for you something of great importance. Look beyond the obvious.

Look deep into what is behind the physical. Look into the metaphysical. There is more to life and existence than everyday human reality. *Explore* the rest of it. *Explore* the spiritual causes, *explore* the spiritual reasons, *explore* the spiritual reality behind what is happening physically. This is what brings the joy that cannot be taken away. This is what brings the love that cannot be lost.'

"And now we are talking to the cells of the eyes, and we are saying to the cells of the eyes, 'Yes, we are aware of cell memory. And we embrace the memory that you, eyes—that in the memory of the cells is the memory of looking upon the face of the one we call Jesus and looking deep into that face and seeing the joy, the love. And when you looked into the eyes and saw the love, you were seeing your Source, that energy that is your essence, that energy of which you are made. And as you think of that white light that you were in and you bring this white light into your eyes, into the cells, into the iris, into the pupils, you think to yourself: 'I can let go of the dysfunctions of the past.'

"All right. Good. We are coming now to the end of hypnosis and we are going to check something with NMR. But at this moment, come up nice and easy. Take a nice deep breath at one...."

"Wow! That was profound!" I said as I stretched and opened my eyes. "So my Essene's life lesson was to look at everything and not be afraid to see everything because that is how we achieve knowledge."

"Yes," Pamela responded, "and knowledge leads to awareness and understanding—otherwise known as consciousness. And raising our consciousness is the reason we're here. It is why our soul is living a human life."

"And his thought that he didn't want to see, in this case the suffering of Jesus, was like a command to the subconscious to program the cells of the eyes not to see clearly. And joy—I've always chased joy but I never had a *clue* where or how to find it. I guess you have to be free to feel joy, and today I learned true freedom comes from understanding the spiritual reasons for what is happening."

"I think you're right." Pamela replied. "As long as we believe, 'I can't be joyful because . . .' or 'I can't be happy because . . .' that's the jail. Okay, so back to the eyes."

With the help of NMR we learned that there was no inner resistance to healing my eyesight and that my subconscious was directing my eyes to heal.

"So my vision will start getting better, right? Amazing!"

"Yes, but don't forget," Pamela said, "there are also physical causes that you must attend to." She gave me exercises to strengthen the muscles around my eyes and exercises to sharpen my near-focus and far-focus vision. She also told me to be sure to blink frequently when reading.

What I learned in this session changed my life profoundly. I learned to look beyond the obvious, to look into the non-physical that is behind the physical. Especially in the case of tragedy and suffering, it is important to explore the spiritual reasons behind what is happening physically. Discovering those reasons brings a joy that cannot be taken away and a love that cannot be lost. It sets you free.

CHAPTER 4

STUCK IN A TROUBLED RELATIONSHIP

So many people end up in relationships that they know for certain are not to their greater good, yet they still cannot leave. Maybe it's a spouse or a family member or a boss or a friend who drives them crazy. Why does this person irritate them so much? Why can't they tell him or her to get lost? They may half-jokingly say they must have known the person in a past life—it's a surprise when they find out it is true. When we find it is true, what can we do about it? The following regression explores the invisible ties that keep individuals bound to each other across lifetimes. However, the session starts out focused not on relationship issues but on a sore arm.

"My right arm is killing me," I complained as I settled into The Chair. "It started right after my last appointment. It feels like a sore muscle or a pinched nerve right up here in the bicep. I have no range of motion, and if I move the wrong way, the pain is killer. Do you think this is a signal of some kind? I've got to do something about this arm!"

"Let's find out," Pamela replied.

NMR disclosed that the pain was a cell memory from my childhood. Pamela had already explained the difference between origin and cause. The origin is the thought or belief that started it. The cause is what triggered it to show up in my present experience. Something happened in my childhood to trigger a cell memory that was being signaled as pain right now, but where did that cell memory come from? I needed to find the origin.

Using NMR, we found the origin was in a life in the third century in what is now Holland. "Oh!" I exclaimed. "I lived in Holland. I have many friends in Holland, and my birth father is Dutch! And you know, the first time I went there I felt like I'd been there before."

Further testing disclosed I was a male in that life, a peasant who worked on the docks, and the origin of my arm pain came from an event in that life. So with the help of Pamela's gentle hypnosis voice, I was off to Holland.

". . . And you become aware of the sounds of the busy docks, the sounds of the docks, the fights that surround, and the smell that is there. Your olfactory senses are very profound. You become aware of the smell of the docks, the sounds and pictures, the sensations. And as you think of this and as you watch this, you become aware of how it would feel to be a male dockworker in the third century in Holland. Are you there, dockworker?"

"Yes."

"And where are you now?"

"At the docks."

"Are you watching or. . . ."

"No. I'm lifting heavy, heavy things."

"Do you lift them by yourself?"

"Right now, yes."

"And how do you like the heavy lifting? Does it feel manly? Does it feel good?" Pamela asks.

"Just heavy. It's my job."

"Are there other dockworkers there with you?"

"Many. And lots of seagulls. The sound is deafening."

"Have you been in this job a long time?"

"It's my life."

"Did you start young?"

"Yes, when I was old enough for the lifting."

"And was it something you were happy to go into?"

"It was just my life. It's what we all did. There wasn't a choice."

"Are you a young man, a middle-aged man?"

"Now I'm in my thirties."

"Do you have a wife?"

"Yes."

"Children?"

"No."

"What's your day like? Do you work all day?"

"Yes. When I leave, people are still working. People come and go."

"Where do you go when you leave work?"

"I go to the tavern with other workers and drink ale."

"Is that a part of the day that you like?"

"It's the best part of the day."

"How late do you stay there?"

"Not late because I go home for dinner."

"Go home for dinner now. Do you walk home alone or with others?"

"We all leave together and go off in our different directions."

"How are you feeling as you walk towards home?"

"Good. I want to go home and see my wife and have dinner."

"As you approach your home, what does it look like?"

"It's a wood house. We have one floor with a large fireplace for heat and for cooking."

"When you come home, is dinner ready?"

"Yes. A big pot of something."

"How does your wife treat you?"

"She just says hello. No hug or anything. Just hello—oh my, she's [my ex-husband] Alex today."

"Are you happy you're home?"

"Yes."

"Let me ask you if this is a good moment to continue on with your life?"

"Yes."

"What are you eating?"

"Vegetables cooked in a pot and some crusty bread."

"Can you see your wife?"

"Yes."

"How does she look?"

"Smaller than most of the other women. I'm not very big. That's why I liked her."

"It must be hard working at the docks if you're not very big."

"I'm strong. But most of the others are taller with bigger shoulders. I'm just not as big as everybody else. But I'm strong."

"What do you feel about your wife as you watch her?"

"I love her, and I'm glad that when I come home she's there. She works hard all day. But she gets home before me and makes the meal. She works for somebody rich. She works in their house. It's not like some of the horrible jobs that other women have to do."

"Does she sit with you to eat your supper?"

"No, but she stands near. She pays attention to me, but she doesn't sit with me. Well, when I finish eating she might sit down."

"Indeed. Finish your meal and tell me what happens next."

"Well, it's dark. There's only light by fire. We sleep. There's nothing else to do. And the day starts early, early, early."

"Do you and your wife fight?"

"Not now."

"Move forward to when there is an argument. Let's see how you argue. Move forward into that argument. You are aware your wife is upset and you are involved in that situation now. Be there at three, two, and one."

"She wants more sex. I'm too tired. All day I lift and I drag and I pull. And I come home and I just want to eat and go to bed. She's upset because there's no sex—or just once in a while."

"How does she show that she's upset?"

"Now she just says she wants more sex. And I tell her I'm just so tired. I'll try. I love her. It's not that I don't love her. I'm just tired. And so I try, and I have sex with her. It's just not very rewarding."

"How does she react?"

"She doesn't know. But I can see now in the future that she's getting angry about it and saying I'm mean and selfish and not considering her needs. And she starts yelling and getting upset. She says she hates our house. It's dark, with a dirt floor. She's mad at me. She just yells and yells and won't let up. And it gets worse. And I don't want to come home so I stay at the pub. And that makes her mad. And when I get home, dinner is cold. And I get mad. And she gets mad. And we fight a lot. We just fight and fight and fight."

"Go to the last fight."

"I push her once. I don't hit her, but I get so angry with her, I push her. She falls down, and she gets really, really angry. She yells and yells and starts pushing me and she pushes me up against the fireplace. I push back because I'm afraid she's going to push me into the fire. She says if I push her one more time, I'll be sorry. And I tell her I don't want to push her, but she's pushing me into the fire. And so she pushes me again. And I push her back.

"And then she grabs something and stabs me in my arm [in the exact place it hurts today]. I see stars. I see red. I'm furious that she did that to me. And I grab her and I shake her and shake her and I just get this rage. I don't even know who I am. And I grab her around the neck. And she's little and my hands are strong from work at the docks. I'm so angry with her. I've been holding it in for so long. The next thing I know she just goes limp.

"I'm holding her up by her neck. And I think, 'Oh my God, I killed her. I'm sorry. I didn't mean to do that. I didn't mean to kill you. You made me so angry. You yell at me. Nothing is ever right. I can't make you happy. But I don't want you dead. I don't want to be with you, but I don't want you dead.'

"Oh, I'm so sorry. I killed her. I can't believe it! It's like letting the air out of a balloon, all that anger and resentment and rage. Mine. I feel it all leave me. I guess killing my wife made me release all that anger. I feel bad I did it, but I feel somehow good, too."

"What happens next?"

"I go get friends and bring them back to the house to take her away. We need to do something with her body. Nobody asks me anything. People are killed all the time in my life. No one is ever punished in my class, so I'm not really afraid of that.

"We've buried her now. I come home and my house is so quiet. I feel relief. And now I really feel the pain in my arm. The muscle in my arm just throbs and throbs. Someone tied something around it to hold the cut together. It's stopped bleeding, but the muscle is just killing me. Oh, it hurts!

"And now I'm not working anymore, and I'm going to the pub but I don't drink. I just go for the company. And I go to the docks to be around my friends. I can't lift much anymore, but they give me something else to do at work. I don't get paid as much, but I'm counting things as they come on and off the ships. My life is so calm now. It's so quiet.

"I feel bad. My wife saw the way rich people live and she wanted that. And she knew she couldn't have it. She blamed me and yelled and yelled at me. And the more she yelled at me, the more I didn't want to have sex with her, and that made her more mad and it just got worse and worse and louder and louder. But now it's so calm and so quiet."

"And then what happens? Move forward into your life."

"There's a group of us. We've all been married, but none of us is married now. Whenever there's time, we do something other than work. We always go together. We have such a good time because nobody is nagging anybody. Nobody is mad at anybody. Nobody has issues with anybody. We'd do anything for each other because we want to and not out of some obligation. It's nice. It's good."

"Does your arm ever heal?"

"The pain goes away. But it's always much weaker than it was before. I can't lift with it. I have to lift everything with my other arm."

"Do you ever think of your wife?"

"At first I did. At first, one minute I'd think, 'Oh, what have I done?' but the next minute I'd think, 'Oh, I love this peace and quiet.' I'm just so thankful for the peace and quiet. I mostly remember the yelling. I try to remember the good times before the yelling started, when I liked coming home. But I got to dread coming home.

"I didn't mean to do it. It just escalated and I killed her, out of rage. She got me so angry. I probably would have shaken her to death if I hadn't grabbed her neck."

"Move to a place now of knowing of that life, where you have left that life and feel yourself in that state of spirit where you're leaving the cares and the worries of life behind you. Tell me the sensations you have in this state of spirit."

"It's nice. I feel light, like I'm weightless. I feel happy, and I see my life as sort of this little scene on a little stage somewhere down there. And I know I shouldn't have killed another person, and I know somewhere sometime I'm going to have to make amends somehow. But the whole village is like on a little stage. And I think, 'Oh, that's so far away. I was in it but I'm not in it anymore.'"

"What was learned? What was gained?"

"Happiness and serenity come from within no matter what is happening around you. You have to make yourself happy."

"What is unfinished about that life, if anything?"

"That I killed her to get the peace and quiet that I wanted."

"You said you would make amends somehow. What does that thought indicate to you now?"

"There are ways to get the serenity you want without killing for it."

"And would you say that this has been learned, that this has been recognized, that this realization is part of your spiritual awareness?"

"Yes. I know this now. We'll have another life together to resolve our differences without murder."

"Good. Move from the spiritual viewpoint into the present life, into the relationship with the one who was then your wife, the one known today as Alex. From your vantage point, what do you see or know that would tell you about the relationship and the letting go of that one now?"

"Well, I let go without killing him—although he says I killed him. That's the issue. He says I destroyed his life, I've destroyed his future, I might as well have just killed him. I know I didn't, but he, probably in his attempt to make me feel guilty, is—most likely without knowing it—speaking from the life where I killed him."

"Yes. He is speaking from that lifetime, too. No future. You killed her. In your awareness now, how would you counsel yourself, from your vantage point, to let go of the guilt?"

"Now that I understand the lesson in this relationship, now that I understand the reason, there's no need for guilt. It would be wonderful if he could learn what I have learned. But I know I am not responsible for his knowledge and understanding.

"Wow!" I exclaimed as I stretched after hypnosis. "So I killed Alex in a past life. That explains why I could never leave. I tried so many times. I could never figure out why I couldn't get away. So it was karma, right? I couldn't leave because I had killed him before and hadn't learned the lesson. And you know what? He and the Dutch wife were so similar!

"I had so many signals to leave. But I didn't know they were signals then. I fell off a step stool while we were painting a new house and tore all the ligaments in my left foot. It was like my body saying, "If you're not going to walk on your path, I'm not going to let you walk at all!" What finally got me to leave was a 19-centimeter abdominal tumor. It was so deep there wasn't even a bulge—even on this skinny body. Fortunately I went to see a psychic before I had surgery. She was also a medical intuitive and she told me this time it was benign, but if I didn't get out of the situation that was causing the stress, next time it would kill me. It took the surgeon hours to get it out because it was stuck to all the organs in my abdomen. My organs were stuck just like I was stuck in that marriage. Recognizing a signal was actually a life-saver.

NMR following the regression confirmed that I had resolved my guilt and felt peaceful about the end of the marriage. I had fulfilled my destiny to learn that lesson, Pamela explained.

"What is the difference between destiny and fate?" I asked. "I want to be clear about destiny and fate."

"Destiny is what you planned before you came into this life. 'This is my plan. This is my purpose. These are my lessons. This is what I want to accomplish. This is the body I'm choosing to accomplish it. I'm choosing the best set-up I can to accomplish this.' Fate is what you actually accomplish while you're here," Pamela explained.

"So," I added, "that's where free will comes in. It's our free will that is the determining factor in fulfilling our destiny. We can either go with the plan or not."

"Yes. And when we don't, that's when things get carried forward to subsequent lives."

My first-century life as an Essene had shown me how an unlearned lesson in a past life can have a physical effect on this life. My third-century Dutch life revealed the effect an unlearned lesson can have on a relationship in this life. Having experienced this much, I knew I couldn't stop until I found all the stories from my past that were affecting my present experience.

CHAPTER 5

THE ORIGIN OF A BIRTH DEFECT

In the few weeks since my first regression, my vision had started to improve. I was doing my eye exercises with diligence, and they were paying off. I now understood why I had such a hard time leaving my ex-husband. Next I wanted to find out about my heart. I was born with a faulty heart. In this regression I learn once again to look beyond the physical cause to find the spiritual lesson of a congenital disorder.

"I was born with a complete heart block," I explained to Pamela. "The electrical charge between the chambers is completely blocked. My pulse has been around 40 my whole life. Fortunately my parents never made me feel limited by it. I just didn't have the wind for anything that required stamina, like swimming or running. But I lived in third-floor walk-ups—which always amazed the doctors—and I ice skated as a kid, walked everywhere when I lived in New York and Amsterdam, and basically ignored it.

"They found the block when I was a year old. I always knew that someday my heart would just give out because it had to work so hard, pumping a double dose of blood with each complete beat. And sure enough, about ten years ago I went into congestive heart failure and had to get a pacemaker.

"Nobody could believe I had lasted fifty-five years. The pacemaker was a good thing, though. I went in for surgery with a pulse of 35 and came out with a pulse of 60. I remember thinking, 'Wow! No wonder people have so much energy! This is great!' So now that I know everything happens for a reason, I want to find out why I have this heart."

"That's quite a story, Ann. Let's see why it happened."

With NMR we learned that the origin was an emotion in a past life in eighteenth-century Boston. I was male, a merchant, and married with two young sons. The emotion was fear, which led to a traumatic death that caused my heart problem today.

I had lived in Boston for nearly two decades in my present life. We tested for the exact address of the house where the merchant had lived so I could find it the next time I was there. It was in Back Bay, an area I knew very well.

"So," Pamela said, "I guess we're going to Boston. Let's begin.

". . . firmly, in that time and place, the sound of your own voice anchoring you very firmly, becoming very aware of yourself in the body you have now in eighteenth-century Boston and saying to me, your feet—are they covered or bare?"

"Oh, covered," a deep voice replied.

"What are you wearing on your feet?"

"Shoes—of beautiful Italian leather."

"Are you indoors or outdoors?"

"Indoors, in my office."

"Tell me about your office."

"There's a large ornate desk and a high-backed wooden chair with rollers on it. There are lots of cases around the room holding my files. They have glass doors on them that move up and down. My office is in the commercial area of Boston."

"Are you alone in your office?"

"Yes, I'm alone. And I'm very worried. I don't know where I'm going to find money. I can't figure out where I've spent my money. There's not enough money to keep going. I don't know where it went."

"Don't you keep careful records?"

"Well, it's not my strongest point. I have people help me with that, but often I tell them things that might mislead them. It started out very well and I was making lots of money. I'm just not quite sure where it went wrong. For so long it was so good.

"I have a wonderful lifestyle. I have a good life. But I can lose it all. I'm very scared. I don't know what's ahead. I could lose everything. I need money to buy inventory to import. I've taken too many draws out of the business to give my family—and myself, I can't say it's all for my family, I love it too—all the finery and servants and carriages and trips."

"What do you import?"

"Silks and things from the East—finery kinds of things— ivory for jewelry and ornate boxes and things like that. They're for people who live my kind of life. Expensive things."

"So here you are in your office, very worried. What are you thinking you will do?"

"I don't know *what* to do. I was going along thinking this money was going to magically appear. I don't know what I was thinking. I just spent myself right into a hole."

"Does anyone else know?"

"No. Which is *awful* because I don't have anyone to talk to about it."

"Do you have sons?"

"Yes. But they're young, ten and twelve."

"So no one to talk to and you don't know what to do. What do you do? Move forward to your next action. What do you do about it?"

"Well, now I'm really in bad shape because I've contacted my suppliers. They have sent me inventory on credit twice, but I haven't been able to pay them and now they won't do it anymore. So now I have nothing to sell. I have no way of keeping my business. And I have some loans that I can't pay.

"I can't face everyone knowing what I've done. It wasn't that I wasn't paying attention; I just did it anyway. I just spent more than I had. I can't face people. Everyone I know is so successful in what they do. Or, who knows? I appear successful, too. Who knows what's really going on with anyone? But I think other people haven't gotten themselves into this mess. I was just totally irresponsible. Oh, how could I have done this? Everything I have will be gone.

"Anything is better than facing this. Anything. My wife is beautiful and young. She'll find someone to take care of her. And my boys, they'll be all right. I just can't tell them. I can't let the world know. I'd rather be dead. They can say whatever they want when I'm dead. It doesn't matter.

"The gun. I have a gun. I've got to do it. I can't think about it. I just have to do it. I'll just get up, go over there to that bookcase, take out the gun, stick it up to my chest, and pull the trigger. That's pretty easy. I don't *think* it will hurt. I think I'll just die. If I hold it right here [I point to my heart] I won't miss and it will make my heart stop and I can't live much longer than that. It *can't* hurt. It won't hurt. And then it will all be over. Nothing will matter anymore.

"Just get up and go over to the bookcase. Put a bullet in the gun. This is such a nice gun. God, what did this cost? Look at this ivory handle—it's *so* beautiful. Nothing that anyone would need. All these things I have, all these objects—you don't *need* them. You just accumulate and accumulate. It's ridiculous. Why did I do this? And now it's *all* gone. All right. Bullet's in. Just put it to your chest and pull the trigger.

[He releases a sigh and laughs.] "It didn't hurt! Oh, what a mess. But it's over. Oh, it's so calm. I can see myself there on the floor all crumpled up. They'll find me. I feel bad for my family, but they'll be okay. There's a whole house of things to sell to live on. Ah, it's so calm, it's so peaceful. I was so worried. My stomach was terrible. It's so calm now."

"What's happening now?" Pamela asks.

"I just feel this incredible calm. I haven't felt like this for so long. Oh, I savor this feeling of feeling so calm. It's so wonderful."

"What do you do now?" Pamela asks.

"I feel like there's somewhere to go. I have to leave this scene. I feel so different now. I feel lightweight, like air. [He chuckles.] I felt so *heavy* and so burdened. Now I just feel like air, like I can float, go wherever I want to go. There are all these other—I don't know what they are. They're like air, too. They're coming towards me and they're saying, 'Come with us. You're going to love it!' I'm just so happy to feel this way. I'll go anywhere. [He laughs.] Take me! Take me! Oh, I love this feeling! I've never felt like this. Ahh, I feel so free!

"There's a huge expanse, so open, like going into the universe or something. It's not dark, though. It's light. It's serenity. Oh, it's so wonderful! I know everyone I left in that life is going to be okay. I don't feel like I hurt them. I mean, I hurt them, but they'll be okay. I know that somehow. I don't know how, but somehow I *know* that.

"Oh, these people here don't care what I had or what I did. They're just saying, 'Come with us, come with us.' They don't really have bodies. They're like floating energy. I feel like I'm in some kind of holding place. I know there's something beyond this. But right now it doesn't matter. Wherever I am right now is just fine with me. There's no guilt, no worry, no problems. I'm staying here for a while."

"Okay," Pamela instructs, "allow yourself to remain in that peaceful calm and move into the guidance and knowledge of your Higher Self. Tell me when you are there."

"There were other solutions," a different voice responds, the Higher Self's voice.

"What other solutions were there?" Pamela asks.

"Take responsibility for his actions. Admit to his failures. He wouldn't face up to his mistakes. He took the easy way out. He didn't need to do that. He left people behind. He didn't give them a chance to forgive him. That's the real pity. He didn't allow himself love and forgiveness."

"Are there any consequences from his actions?"

"He's calm and peaceful now because he's not worried. But he must un-create his actions in another physical life."

"Move forward now in your awareness to when the time has come to figure out how to rectify that. Tell me what is happening."

The Higher Self continued, "In order to *receive* forgiveness, one must learn how to forgive, especially oneself. Just as to receive love, one must be able to give love. He was unable to do that. He was loved without experiencing the joy of being loved. He did not experience joy because he was not aware of his inner light, the power of his spirit. That is what the soul must learn—to connect with the power of the spiritual self, to give and receive love and be joyous, and to take responsibility for one's actions and be forgiving of self and others. That is what it will take to un-create taking his physical life. That is his soul lesson."

"How is this choice made? When is the next life?" Pamela asks.

"Not long" is the reply. "Things will be more modern—more advanced technology. The lesson might be better learned if the life is lived as a female. She will be born to someone who will not stay with her so that she can learn to forgive the rejection by understanding it. And she will need to learn to give and receive love."

"Thank you. Think now of the body of that merchant," Pamela instructs. "Such a mess, you said, that gentleman's heart. Send healing energy to it. Pour into that heart your light and ask it to forgive you as though you were talking right there to those cells. Ask that they receive this healing light as your attempt to ask for their forgiveness.

"See in your mind's eye that heart becoming whole again, healing from the shock and trauma. Holding it in your hands, you put it back together. Removing the bullet, soothing the heart, you tell it that you understand now the consequences, that never, ever again will you harm the heart in that manner or harm the heart at all.

"Tell the heart you will dedicate yourself to bringing it love and joy so it feels love and joy deeply, completely. For the one that the heart served has now recognized the importance of that life and the lessons learned and gained. And the heart feels honored and feels it lived a worthy life and served you well. It has, at long last, gained recognition.

"As you move again back into that light of your spirit, you now find your spirit, your Higher Self, hovering over your physical body as Ann. You can feel your Higher Self sending its light to you even as *you* shine that light on your physical heart today.

"Your soul says to that physical heart, 'I understand, and I am asking the cells of the heart to embrace my desire to act upon my word. I seek your forgiveness, for I do truly recognize now how important the heart is physically and symbolically, how important life and love and joy are to the soul and to the physical being.' You say to your heart, 'It is my intent to embrace life with joy, it is my intent to feel love, which for you is the most life-giving tonic of all.'

"You recognize how powerful it is to have this team working together—the power of the body to heal, the power of the spirit to supply healing energy and life force and to gain knowledge, and the power of the mind to record it all and, with its perfect memory, to continue to direct the healing to its completion.

"As you focus on healing in the future, your thought as you talk to the subconscious is one of gratitude and joy. 'I thank you for doing your part. Without you, I could not be on this spiritual path. I thank you, heart, for your forgiveness. I reassure you, heart, that I will never jeopardize you again.'

"Embracing your own power, embracing your positive awareness of self, take a nice deep breath now, Ann, and slowly I will count from one to five as you come out of hypnosis. . . ."

I was back. "So that personality of my soul shot himself in the heart," I exclaimed, "and I came into this life with a messed-up heart. Amazing! Is that usually the case? When people are born with a defect, does it usually come from something like that in a past life?"

"More often than not," Pamela replied. "Congenital disorders usually come from a past life. Of course sometimes something happens in utero, but there's a metaphysical reason for that physical development, too."

We had discovered the non-physical reason for my heart block, but I was curious to know the physical cause too. With NMR we learned it was the result of my birth father being gassed in World War II. Maybe that was why he was chosen to be my birth father. We tested further and discovered he also had two sons after the war and one of them was born with the same heart condition.

"So," I commented, "it's the metaphysical reasons—the spiritual reasons—that allow us to make sense of everything in our lives. And the Higher Self even recommended adoption in my next life so I could learn to forgive. That's a pretty good case for pre-life planning. So before each life we plan our lessons, our purpose, and even choose the parents and other people and circumstances that will best help us to fulfill the purpose and learn the lessons in that life. That's why you said *nothing* is arbitrary, everything happens for a reason.

"I kind of hate to admit this," I went on, "but until recently I was pretty reckless with money. I can't even begin to count the number of times I looked at my bank balance and asked myself where all the money went. And that was exactly what my Boston guy said.

"I'm a little confused about forgiveness. Everybody's so keen on forgiveness. But is it really forgiveness? Isn't it more about understanding? If you understand why something happened, that it was all part of a soul's plan to learn a lesson, then there really isn't anything to forgive. Of course, that's if you're looking at the non-physical reasons."

"You make a good point," Pamela replied.

"And so much for judgment—how can you judge anyone when they're just working out a lesson? This puts a whole new spin on things. I'm beginning to understand what it means to be an observer of your life. It doesn't mean not being involved in it. It means seeing things from your soul's perspective. That's really the only way you can understand what is truly going on.

"So my Boston man couldn't experience joy because he wasn't aware of his inner light, the power of his spirit. But that's everyone's universal soul lesson, right? And his individual lesson was to take responsibility for his actions and trust in the love and forgiveness of others. By learning this, he was able to un-create taking his physical life and now my heart can begin to heal."

After this regression, NMR revealed that I would have to heal my ability to love and be loved before I could heal my heart. My next regression to the past would start me on that path. Over time I worked very hard to heal my heart but nothing happened. Then I learned with NMR that my one-year-old had overheard the doctor tell my mother, "Nothing can be done." So we regressed to her and Pamela helped her understand that although doctors are very smart, sometimes they can be wrong. And, for every rule there is an exception and she was an exception to the doctor's rule. Once my infant believed something could be done, I was able to begin manifesting a stronger heart.

Chapter 6

ADOPTION: WHO REALLY CHOOSES WHO?

Adoption is a difficult experience for a child. No matter how loving the adoptive parents are and how wonderful a life they provide, at some level the child still feels unwanted, unloved, and unworthy of love. So what is the role of adoption in a soul's plan? In this regression I learn everything I ever wanted to know about adoption—the spiritual reasons, the lessons, and the opportunities it provides. This is my first regression to an inner, or earlier, age of myself in this life rather than to a past life personality.

"The issue," I began, "that probably has had the most impact on my life is being adopted. Don't get me wrong. I had great parents and have a great life. But as I get older I can see I've never trusted relationships. I was always the one who left so I wouldn't be the one left. I know I've been emotionally unavailable my whole life, even as a child. I never let myself feel anything for fear of being hurt."

Pamela and I used NMR to test for programs I might have taken on in my childhood, such as feeling unworthy of love and feeling unwanted.

"You know, Ann, children that are adopted into very, very loving homes—it isn't that they're not getting the love, it's that they feel unworthy of it and so they're blocking the love. I would say that seems to be what we have happening here."

We continued on with NMR, looking for emotions. We found some: I was unhappy in the womb. I was angry and felt shame. I thought there was something wrong with me and that I was making my mother unhappy. And I felt rejected.

"So, in the very beginning, Ann, you're already thinking, 'Maybe if I was better....'"

"Yeah, growing up I always thought to myself, 'Whatever you do, don't rock the boat so they don't send you back.'"

"Exactly," Pamela added. "If my mother is going to give me away just for who I am, these people will too, unless I'm really making nice. That's a very heavy feeling, a very heavy emotion."

More NMR revealed that my birth was difficult because I was struggling *not* to get out. "See, as long as you're *in* mom," Pamela explained, "she can't do anything about it. As soon as you're *out* of mom, now what? What will happen to me then?"

"Is that what breech births are about?" I asked. "The fetus doesn't want to be born?"

"Often, yes," was the answer. "So are there any other programs you want to check before we begin?"

"Where are we going?" I asked.

"To the fetus in this life. That's where the emotions are."

"My fetus? How can my fetus talk?"

"She will communicate mentally, and the subconscious mind will speak her thoughts."

"Will I talk or act like a baby?"

"Some people do, some people don't. Some prefer to keep more of a mental or emotional distance from an inner self, which is what all the inner ages are. To do that, people unconsciously direct their subconscious mind to act as a translator for the inner self by conveying the emotions, energy, and attitude of the inner self through tone of voice and descriptive phrases—although just hearing what an inner self is thinking and feeling can trigger an emotional response in the present self. Sometimes an adult's inner child will use phrases the adult self finds hard to believe a child would know or use. I always say you never know what a child, including an inner child, has picked up mentally from older kids and adults. And again, when the subconscious is acting as a translator, it may speak in the language of the adult self in an attempt to help the adult self more clearly grasp the thoughts, feelings, and attitude of the child one was."

We did more NMR and learned I did not trust love, I did not trust emotions. I also believed that my mother gave me away because she didn't want me. We asked if there was anything else I needed to know before the regression, and the answer was no.

During the hypnosis induction I experienced my body getting smaller and smaller until I was that little embryo in the womb. (The transcript of this induction is one of the sample inductions at the back of the book.) When Pamela asked me to go to the sad feelings, a weepy, scared little voice responded, "I'm all alone here. I'm just floating around in here and I'm *all* alone. There's nobody."

"No one at all?" Pamela asked.

"I feel like I'm in here all by myself."

"Does your mommy know you're there?"

"Yeah."

"What did she think when she found out?"

"She was afraid. She thought, 'Oh no, this can't be. I'm married to someone else. This is terrible.'"

"What did you think as you heard mom thinking that?"

"That I was terrible."

"You know what, baby girl? I know this is very hard to understand, but when mom says this is terrible, she means it's terrible for *her* that she has a baby in her body. She doesn't mean *you're* terrible. I'll tell you something about humans. Are you listening, baby girl?"

"Yes."

"Good. Well, it would be *wonderful*, baby girl, if every single mommy and daddy were so happy and so thrilled that a baby was coming. Now you would *think* that would be so because they do things to have babies come. But they aren't always prepared or ready for that. Can you imagine that? Sometimes they're very shocked, very upset that there's a baby. And I'll tell you some of the reasons. I'll tell you the very reason for you, okay?"

"Uh-huh."

"Your mommy and your daddy—do you know anything about your daddy right now? Let's see if you remember your conception. Would you do that for me *before* I tell you what's going on here with your mommy?"

"Uh-huh."

"Okay. Think back. Your legs and arms will get smaller and smaller until they disappear. And your body disappears until you're just in this little egg. And you can be inside the egg or outside the egg. You can go in and out! We're going right back to the moment of your conception, to when this egg began to grow. And now we're going back just a little bit farther. Where are you? Are you inside or outside the egg?"

"I'm not in."

"You're not in. All right. Then you're spirit right now. And are you aware of your mommy? See if you can find her. Maybe you see her energy. Look for your mommy and daddy. And begin to let that picture open for you. Mommy and daddy are together and you're in the spirit form, but you can see with your spirit, sense where they are and what's happening. Now the impression begins to gather. Are mommy and daddy inside or outside a building?"

"Inside."

"And are they talking softly or loudly?"

"Not loud."

"Can you hear their words? Can you make sense of them?"

"No."

"Is the sound of their voices pleasant?"

"Uh-huh."

"Okay. You know, you can tell what's going on in their minds. Whose mind do you want to get into, daddy's or mommy's?"

"Mommy's."

"Okay. So get into mommy's thoughts. What is she thinking?"

"I'm lonely."

"So mommy's feeling lonely. And what is she feeling with the presence of this man here? Is she happy with him being here?"

"Uh-huh."

"Okay. How's her body feeling? Can you tell from her thoughts? Is she having pleasant feelings?"

"Yeah."

"So it's a happy situation. She's okay with this?"

"Uh-huh. I mean, she's feeling like she shouldn't be there, but...."

"But she's liking it?"

"Yeah."

"Why do you think she's feeling like she doesn't belong there?"

"'Cuz she's got a husband. But she's lonely. And it's so nice. He has his arms around her and it just feels really nice."

"What's he feeling?"

"Same thing. He's lonely, too."

"Oh. And why are you here, spirit?"

"Because these two are going to be my parents."

"How do you have this knowing?"

"Because I decided that they're going to be my parents."

"Go back to when you decided. Just let yourself drift with that thought back to when you decided *these two* would be your parents. Where are you? Are you alone? Are there others?"

"No, there are others. They're helping me plan things."

"What draws you to these two as parents?"

"It's for something I have to learn. I have to have parents that are going to help me learn my lesson."

"And how do you know these two are the ones who will do that?"

"Because they're not married and they'll have to give me away. And I have to get to my other parents."

"That's right. It's *all* part of a plan, a very important plan. And the reason it had to happen this way was because you needed to be the child of parents who couldn't have their own babies. So somebody had to have the baby *for* them. So *she* didn't reject *you*. In a sense *you* rejected *her*. So it was *your* power that made all this unfold because you didn't want to be raised by this mommy and daddy. That's not what you wanted—or it would have happened that way, because the universe does *not* make mistakes. And what do you plan to accomplish in this lifetime that you are going to live?"

"Learn about rejection. It's going to help me to realize myself in a spiritual way. But I have to overcome the human stuff to get there. So this will be a good way to teach me many lessons about my own strength. It doesn't have to come from other people."

"Very good. Then moving back to the womb where you are floating around feeling so alone, what is mommy thinking?"

"There's no way she'd get rid of me, kill me. She doesn't believe in that. So she's going to give birth to me and give me away. She tells me she loves me even though she can't keep me. But still, it's so lonely in here 'cuz I don't know what's going to happen to me. And she's got such mixed-up feelings about me. She keeps saying, 'I love you, I just can't keep you.'"

"So let's talk to you now, baby. Hearing your mommy saying she loves you but she can't keep you, is this confusing to you?"

"Yeah. I think if she loves me, how could she not keep me? I mean, there's gotta be a way."

"There may well be a way. But your mommy isn't seeing that way. Your mommy is married to a man other than your daddy, and your mommy is afraid if he finds out he'll leave her. And she's afraid to be alone with a baby girl without a husband. So your mommy has two problems: she loves you, and she is afraid. And her fear is stronger right now, wouldn't you say?"

"Uh-huh."

"What's really important for you to hear, baby, is that she hasn't met you yet, has she? She doesn't know anything about you yet."

"Well she knows I'm part of her and this guy, my father. And she really did like him."

"Yes, she would love to keep you for that reason."

"Yeah."

"But she's *afraid* to. And something about people that you need to know is that sometimes they let things like fear stop them from doing what they really want to do. Maybe your mother would really like to keep you, but she's too afraid. And maybe she thinks she would be doing you a big favor—that she loves you enough to see to it that you have a mommy and a daddy who are married and together so you have a family. If she keeps you, then she's afraid you won't have a daddy because her husband will leave her. So you won't have a mommy *and* a daddy. She's afraid she won't be able to take care of you properly. Do you think that's going on in her head?"

"Yeah."

"So it's important for you, baby girl, to know that *there's nothing wrong with you.* You aren't bad. You aren't wrong. In fact, you belong here or you wouldn't *be* here. Did you listen to when the spirit part of you said it knew this was going to happen and that it was important for this to happen?"

"Yes."

"You're part of that. You're experiencing that. It's important for you to be able to *feel* your mother's love for you. Even though you know she's so afraid, she wants so much for you to have a family that she is going to give you away. But it's also important for you to know what's going to happen to you. Do you remember, baby girl, where you come from?"

"You mean from the spirits?"

"Yes. Remember that?"

"Yes."

"And do you remember the light all around you when you were in spirit?"

"Yes."

"Do you know where that light is now?"

"No."

"Okay. Spirit of this baby girl, she needs you. You need to be with this baby girl and be part of this baby girl's body so that I can say to this baby girl, 'The light that you come from is inside you, it's right there with you.'"

"Then I won't feel so alone."

"That's right! Not only do you feel its presence loving you, but you can talk to it. And it will talk back to you."

"It's like having a friend in here with me."

"Yes it is! So ask that light inside there with you, 'What will happen to me after I'm born?' What does it tell you?"

"That I'm going to be taken care of and I'm going to have everything I need. My new parents are going to really love me and it's going to be okay. I'm going to get a good deal!"

"When you hear this, baby girl, from that light, do you feel calmer?"

"Well, it makes it not so scary. Everything feels calmer because I'm not so afraid."

"Good. Move forward to when birth is beginning and tell me what happened at your birth. Tell me what happened when you were born. How do you know it's time?"

"Well I've been ready to go ever since my spirit came to me and was with me. I haven't been afraid. I've been ready to go! I just had to get big enough so I could go."

"Are you big enough now?"

"Yeah, I'm big enough now. I want to go, but I want to stay with her because she's my mother. But I'm not afraid of going anymore. I'm ready. I guess I want to go more than I don't want to go. So I just say it's time to go.

"I'm going through this tunnel thing. And then when I'm out, somebody hits me. That hurt! I didn't like that. Then someone takes me and wraps me up and cleans me off and puts me in this bin. I want to see what my mother looks like from the outside, and she's trying to see me. But all I see is really dark hair.

"Everybody's making a fuss and taking care of me. Actually, they do hold me and rock me. But it's like these strangers are holding me. It would have been nice if they had given me to her to hold me and rock me so I could have felt the outside of what I felt the inside of."

"Yes, that would have been nice. Why don't you, there in your bin, baby girl, close your eyes. I'm going to ask you, adult Ann, to be there at your birth, as the adult. I want you to be there to catch the baby as it comes through the birth canal and hold her. Be right there at the birth canal.

"And now, baby girl, as you see that opening, it's light, it's full of light, now in that next push, that's it, use all your strength to push, push, push. And as you come out, go right into those arms.

"Now, adult Ann, look down into your arms. There's a beautiful, beautiful baby girl there. Look into her eyes. See that intelligence, that spirit in her eyes. See who she is. Notice how perfectly formed she is. Touch her and tell her how beautiful she is and how important she is to you.

"Hold that little newborn baby next to your heart so she can feel your heart beating with love for her. Place your hand over her heart and tell her she is loved, she is wanted, everything is going to be all right, that she was born for *you*, and that you are thanking her mother for carrying her safe and sound and for keeping her body so perfectly so that now, this precious gift is *yours*. Touch her skin. Stroke it. Baby girl, feel your skin being touched and stroked. That's it. Baby girl, that's the human touch. That's the touch of love, that gentle, loving, stroking feeling.

"And the baby girl feels loved, feels that light inside her is completely surrounding her and is loving her and giving her that human touch through the grown-up you. And that baby girl recognizing, 'You are not alone. You are *always* loved. This love surrounds you always. It's right there inside you, and when you want to feel it you just ask that it surround you as it is right now, now that you feel completely and totally contented, wanted, loved. And every single part of you feels you're perfect.'

"That's what you're doing, grown-up Ann. You're looking at this baby girl and you are thinking and you are saying right to her, 'You are *perfect.*' She is. She's absolutely perfect just as she is. This whole moment is perfect. This whole life is perfect. It all unfolds perfectly. You set your plan, you stuck to your plan, and your plan is unfolding exactly as you scripted it.

"You recognize it is in this body that you will be coming to terms with those important things you set out to do. You will be healing. You will be healing your ability to love and be loved. And symbolically you will be healing the heart, too—literally as well, because the heart is symbolic of love and in a past long ago time you harmed yourself in the heart because you didn't trust in love.

"In this life you are learning to trust in self, to trust in your light, to trust in the love that you have to give to yourself, and to trust in the love of that light that is the essence of *all* spirit, of *all* souls.

"With that recognition, now let us ask that the subconscious bring forward the directors of the mental and emotional programming. And on the screen of your mind you see written the belief: 'I am not wanted.' By erasing that now, the programmers are told: 'Remove this belief, this thought, this program.'

"And now you see written: 'I am wrong. I don't belong here. My mother rejected me.' Now you erase those. As they disappear, as they fade away, your directors of your belief system are altering those beliefs and moving into the new thinking. Your human is recognizing the changes taking place.

"And now, you write on that screen of your mind: 'I am wanted. I belong here. I am perfect. I am loved. My mother made a great sacrifice because of her love for me.' Good. And you shine those golden and bright, which tells your programmers this is the new belief, the new thinking. And then you reinforce it by thinking to yourself again, with great joy: 'I belong here. I am loved—always—just for being me. I am perfect. I accept myself. And others accept me, too. I love my body. I love my heart. My body is perfect for me.' Good.

"And now as I count from five to one...."

I was back. I felt both exhausted and exhilarated. "I really got emotional there," I commented. "I could feel all that loneliness that I've felt all my life just ... evaporate. It really got me that my light is always with me and I'm never alone. It feels so good to have that knowing.

"And when my newborn was held and caressed and heard all those loving things, it was so emotional. I'll never forget that. I really felt loved. What a magnificent feeling! I'm getting all teary just thinking about it. And my spirit wasn't in the egg. What was that about?"

"The spirit doesn't necessarily ride out the entire gestation," Pamela answered. "It *would* be pretty boring, wouldn't it? So it comes and goes. It even comes and goes for the first several months after the physical birth."

"What?" I exclaimed. "You know, I've always thought newborns must be pretty bored. In fact, the few I've been around, I've always told them—mentally, of course—that it *does* get better. Eventually they'll get to run around and *do* things, so they should just hang in there.

"And I feel like I have to tell all adopted people about planning it ourselves. That's huge! It certainly takes care of feeling rejected. We masterminded it! Now *that* is life changing!"

I experienced so many changes after this regression. This might sound sappy, but I did really start to feel love all around me. And I started to feel lovable and worthy and okay as I am. When I transcribed this tape, hearing Pamela ask my adult self to let my newborn know she was perfect and she was loved made me tear up all over again. It still makes me weepy.

As each of my distressed inner ages came forward in subsequent regressions, Pamela would help them feel the comfort and love and protection of their light, their spirit. And the adult me was beginning to feel it as well.

Chapter 7

THE PERILS OF IGNORING INTUITION

How often have I said to myself, "If only I'd followed my intuition?" I know I'm not alone in this. When we look back at those messages after the fact, we can see that they were right. Ignoring our intuition always comes at a price. This past life personality's story demonstrates what can happen when fear keeps us from listening to our inner guidance.

I want to find out about my toenail," I began. "I've never had one on the third toe of my right foot. It's been a nuisance my whole life. The nail bed is extremely sensitive, and if anyone drops anything within ten feet of me, it's always on that toe. I literally see stars."

NMR revealed that the origin of the lack of a toenail was in a twelfth-century life in Florence. I was female, happily married to a merchant, with two children and another on the way. I lived a full life for those times—I was an artist, painting was my hobby—but I died of internal injuries after falling from a horse. A flash of insight during NMR—by now I knew to regard such an insight as a message from my Higher Self—told me to ask if the horse had stepped on my toe, and the answer was yes. This was the reason for my missing toenail. Now I had to find out what it was signaling.

"Now I already have a mental picture of this whole story, so how do I know when I go into hypnosis that my conscious mind isn't making this up?" I asked.

"When we're doing the NMR, Ann, you're in a very focused state of concentration—at least the way we do it you are—and that is an altered state, a state of hypnosis. So as the subconscious is talking about it, you're tuning in and seeing it. That's psychic awareness. You are in a slightly altered state."

We tested further with NMR and found that the visuals I was getting about this life were accurate. My horse had tripped, I fell off, and the horse fell on me. My unborn child died in the accident. My husband in that life is my brother in this life. And my unborn child in that life was my birth mother in this life.

"Oh! Rejection! Rejection!" Pamela exclaimed.

"Yeah, I rejected her then, and she rejected me in this life. Interesting!"

Having experienced six inductions, it was taking less time for me to get into an altered state. Now I could close my eyes, take a few deep breaths, roll my eyeballs upwards, watch the numbers beginning from 100 and counting backward disappear into blackness, and with some help from Pamela to relax my body, *voila*! I was there. Soon I was drifting back through time to twelfth-century Italy.

". . . Now, very aware of that woman in twelfth-century Florence, you are her, thinking her thoughts, feeling her feelings. You become aware of what surrounds you, looking around and noticing what you see. You become aware of your own self, of your own body, even of the clothing you have on. When you respond to this voice that is speaking to you in your head, the sound of your own voice makes the sights that surround you clearer and clearer, makes the sounds that surround you clearer and clearer. My first question to you is, 'What *do* you see? What *is* around you?'"

"I'm in a house, an empty house. We're moving into this house. There's another baby coming. The walls are being painted white, and there are lots of pictures that are going to go up on the walls—my pictures, pictures I painted. So we're painting the walls white."

"What kind of pictures do you paint?"

"Scenes with flowers and scenes of the city and the people in it, scenes of children—lots of little children are in the pictures. I paint what's around me. I try to reproduce what I see every day because I have a happy life, so my paintings are happy. My husband likes my paintings.

"It's fun, it's exciting. We're having a new baby and moving into this house. It's a little bigger than our old house and it's a nice house and I just have a really nice life. I don't really have any worries. My children are beautiful. They're little; they're pretty little. I like being a mother. I just have a really nice life."

"Good! It sounds very lovely. What are you wearing today?"

"A dress with long sleeves."

"And as you are standing there, close your eyes and feel the fabric of your skirt. Beneath the skirt, are your legs bare or are you wearing something on your legs? Can you feel the fabric of your skirt?"

"The fabric is medium weight. My legs are bare. It's spring. There is a lot of sunlight coming in through the windows."

"And as you go deeper within yourself you begin to move now," Pamela instructs. "You move forward in that spirit and in that body to a moment in which an important life lesson is unfolding, a life lesson *very* important to your spirit, to your soul. You will feel it, you will be a part of it, you will experience it as it is happening. At three, at two, at one, what is your body seeing, what is your body feeling?"

"My body feels good. I'm carrying a baby and that's no problem. I feel excited. Physically I feel good. It's early in the pregnancy. I'm just getting a little stomach—you're just starting to be able to see it. The children are at home with their grandparents, and my husband and I are going riding outside the city. It's so much fun being with him and doing things with him. We've been married for a while, but we still act like we just met. We love to get away together, just us. We go out to the woods and have a picnic and act like we are still dating. It's really, really fun.

"So we go to the edge of the city to where they keep the horses. We go there every Sunday and we get our horses. One of us has a new horse, though. One of our regular horses—there's something wrong with it. My husband takes the new horse. No, *I* take the new horse because his horse is a little feisty and he doesn't think I should be on his horse. So I take the new horse. They promise me that this horse is very gentle and responds well to commands and I won't have *any* problems with it at all.

"For a moment I think I shouldn't be getting on a new horse while I'm pregnant. But I don't want to disappoint my husband so I say okay. It's a really nice horse. I feed it an apple and stroke it and get familiar with it. So we mount the horses and ride off down the trail in the hills outside of Florence. It's a beautiful, beautiful day. There are other people around, either on horses or walking. Some are sitting under the trees having picnics. And we're riding and we're riding. There are trees along the trail, and their branches form an arch above us.

"My husband is ahead of me on the trail and something happens and his horse rears. Now his horse reared once before and my old horse, it didn't bother her at all. But my new horse gets spooked and rears. As it rears it hits something, the branch of a tree or something. It all happens so fast, but it hits something. And the force throws me off the horse onto the edge of the path.

"My horse loses its balance and comes down on me, it just crashes down on me. It's scrambling and scrambling to get up, and as it gets up, one of its big horrible hooves crashes down on my foot and then its whole body falls on me.

"My husband jumps down and comes over and yells my name over and over and asks me if I am all right. I feel like I have just been smooshed. I must have passed out because that's all I remember. I just remember I hit the ground and saw this huge animal coming at me, falling down on me. And that was it. I passed out.

"I wake up in the old house. My husband is there with two other men and two women. At first I don't know who they are. As I wake up my husband is holding on to me and holding my hand and calling to me. And I ask what happened, and he tells me that we were riding and my horse fell on me, do I remember? I say I do and ask who these people are. He tells me they are doctors and nurses. They have been watching me. I've been asleep for over a day and I'm badly hurt. I have a lot of hurt on the inside. And I ask about the baby, and he says we lost the baby. The baby's gone; the baby couldn't survive the crash of the horse on it.

"I get very upset because I wanted that baby. I wanted another of his babies. He tells me I have to be strong because I have a lot of injuries and I'm bleeding inside and I need to use my mind to get better. He tells me, 'You have to will yourself to get better because you have two other children and you don't want to leave *those* children. We can have another baby. But you have to really focus on getting better.' And I say, 'I will, I will.' But then every day, the pain is just *horrible*.

And they keep giving me stuff for the pain but it knocks me out. I try my hardest to get better and to tell my body to get better, but I just keep getting weaker and weaker.

"My boys come into the room, but I can't really talk to them. I certainly can't be a mother to them. I just get weaker and weaker. And everyone is around me, but I have no strength and I just let go. The boys are little. They think I fell asleep. They don't really know what is going on.

"My husband is really upset, and I watch them all from above as they realize I've stopped breathing. It's sweet, you know? I love my husband so much and we had one of those once-in-a-millennium kind of marriages. It was perfect. I say to him, 'I'll always be with you. I'm not with you physically, but I'll come to you all the time. Don't be sad. I have no pain. I'm going to a great place and I'll be with you.' And he hears me.

"There is lots of light. I know that's where I want to go. I know I can still watch and still communicate and be with them, so that's what I do. And it is quite nice. I *am* sorry that I couldn't have spent more time in the physical world with my husband and my children because our life was idyllic. It was the perfect life. And if that horse hadn't freaked out I could have just lived on and on and had more children and grandchildren. But you can't blame the horse. It just reacted.

"I'm happy. But I was sad to leave. I was really sad to leave that physical situation, that physical body, that physical life."

"Do you have a question in your mind, then," Pamela asked, "*why* such an idyllic, perfect life should be cut short and leave two boys without a mother and a loving husband without his wife? Go to where you can discover why. Ask this of yourself, 'Why? *Why* could I not get better when I tried my best? *Why* did this happen and why could I not recover from it?' Ask that question and then allow yourself to receive the answer. And report on that answer as it comes into your thoughts."

"It was too perfect. It was too good. Maybe it was the experience of everything being perfect. There wasn't anything to learn, to overcome, or to resolve. Maybe that was the lesson: you *can* have a life like that."

"Why you? Your husband was happy too. Why didn't he die?"

"I didn't listen to my inner voice that told me not to get on the new horse. I was pregnant and should not be riding a new horse. But I ignored my inner voice because I didn't want to disappoint my husband. He loved our Sunday rides so much. I didn't want to disappoint him."

"Well, then, we have some testing we will do regarding this. But for the moment perhaps you can take that wonderful life force that the spirit has after leaving the body and pour light into the cells of the body it has left so that the cells have memory of being restored back into that perfect pattern of energy, forming that perfect pattern for the body. The arms healing from the cellular level, the heart, the lungs, every part of the body that was crushed. Now, as you are pouring the light in, at the energy level of the cells, order is restored.

"And even in that foot, in that third toenail, restoring the toe and the nail of the toe to what it was before, into that perfect pattern of nail and flesh and muscle and bone and tendons and ligaments—restoring all of them to their perfect state. And as you're doing so you say, 'Yes, from this level of consciousness I do indeed have the power to restore the body although I have left the body, although the life force has left because the need for the body has passed. The body can be restored and honored so that I can think of that body as whole and complete so it matches that lifetime, a perfect formation.

"As you think that thought and you move into the present, you see on that screen of your mind where old programs appear and where you direct the changes in the programming, you see the thought: 'No matter how hard I try, I cannot heal my body.' And that thought is erased, that belief system is erased, and you replace it with: 'In higher understanding and awareness from the higher levels of my consciousness, I can heal the cells and the form and the structure of my body.' And you write: 'I allow it to be so.'

"And now you bring forward the thought: 'If everything is too perfect, something disastrous will happen.' Erase that and in its place put: 'Everything is perfect in all that occurs. All unfolds perfectly, and I rejoice at this realization. The universe is perfect, and it is good, and happiness is to be enjoyed, embraced. And from my happiness I can share and teach and give.'

"And as you allow those positive changes to begin occurring, at one hypnosis is over...."

"That was a good one!" I exclaimed. "You know, I've never liked being close to horses. I don't mind them from far away and I love watching them run, but I've never liked being close to them."

"I guess now you know why," Pamela laughed. "So today's regression, like the first one to your Essene, is an example of a past life where you needed to look at the overall view. But we need to go back to this life because now you need to go into the emotional aspects. Why didn't she listen to her intuition? What was the fear?"

We checked some programs using NMR. In my current life I was fearful of perfection, but [through the work I was doing with Pamela] that program was already changing. This came as quite a surprise. I had no awareness of this program, but on reflection I could see how it manifested in my life. I also believed I couldn't heal my own body, but this also was changing. I was physically healing many things, and I now believed I could heal my toenail.

After this regression, my toenail grew in very quickly several eral times but it always fell off. I asked my body why and learned that my Florence housewife was still in distress. A subsequent regression revealed why she had ignored her intuition. Her six-year-old came forward. Her daddy had left her, and although she knew he was in heaven, she was certain she had done something wrong to make him go away; she must have disappointed him. Pamela helped her understand she hadn't disappointed him. With this new awareness she now understood that the fear of disappointing her husband had kept her from heeding her intuition—and I was able to grow a permanent toenail.

CHAPTER 8

THE SOUL LESSONS OF SEXUAL ABUSE

Millions of people are sexually or emotionally abused, neglected, or suffer some kind of trauma as children. Some bury these memories and cannot recall them. Others keep these memories in their conscious minds and live with them every day. Either way, these memories impact their lives. They can shut down their emotions, assuming that if they don't feel, they can't be hurt. They don't trust people or relationships. Healing such trauma may seem beyond hope. But there is hope. It is possible to heal, as the next five regressions show.

For the past few days I've had a throbbing feeling in my right arm like someone grabbed it too hard," I said as I settled into The Chair. "The pain isn't intense, but it hurts. It must be a signal, and I'm eager to find out what it is." Without thinking about it, I surprise myself by suddenly blurting out, "You know, up until I was a teenager, I was chronically constipated."

Pamela's hands flew onto my ankles to do the NMR testing—which revealed that I had been sexually abused as a young child.

"When there are negative thoughts and programs that hold us back, it's important to change them. The reason we work with issues like sexual abuse is because it's very difficult to alter old programs when there are inner ages that are fiercely holding onto them. And sexual abuse tends to imprint a lot of that negative thinking. Trying to change negative thinking when there is an inner age stuck in negative thinking only serves to upset them, making them furious."

Pamela suggested we test with NMR to see if I had what she called a Punisher. I did.

"Most of us are taught through punishment," Pamela explained. "Few parents, certainly when we were growing up, were evolved enough to say, 'Well, that was an interesting choice. Let's examine the consequences of this choice. Now you have to sit in your room for an hour without watching your favorite TV program. So was that really the best choice? You think about it and we'll discuss it when you come out.' Most parents just yell and sometimes hit. Punishment. You're sitting in your room because you're being punished because you were bad.

"So if we want to be good, we tend to develop an internal mechanism that punishes us when we're bad. This gets complicated because so many things that we're taught in childhood are bad we later discover are not. Even worse, many children don't have the sophistication to separate, 'what I did was bad' from 'I'm bad.' And if they get enough punishment, enough of that 'I'm bad' message, their Punisher will be eternally punishing them according to their own programs.

"If you have a program that money is bad and you have a Punisher, then you're not going to get money. If you have a program that money is bad and you have money, then you're going to be punished for having money. It gets quite complex, which is why it's important to check for programs from childhood that are getting in our way. So to dismantle the Punisher we need to convince the part of us that felt we needed a Punisher—the subconscious—why we do not."

"Well, I want mine gone," I insisted. "Let's do it."

"Okay," Pamela instructed, "lean back and mentally think: I understand why in my parents' day and age they felt discipline meant punishing. That's how they were raised and that's how society did it. So they spanked and they punished, and that was how they thought you had to keep children in line. Well, I don't think that any more. I think there's a more enlightened way. I think rather than punishing a child you can help the child understand the consequences of her choices.

"So I don't need the Punisher anymore. I have guidance now. I can ask my Higher Self if something is for my highest good or not. I don't need the Punisher to keep me in line anymore. I'm not a child anymore. I have a means of discovering what is good and what is bad. The Punisher's job is ended, and I'm going to go into my creative levels and I'm going to take away the energy I've used to create the Punisher and I'm going to erase 'I need to be punished.' I'm going to replace it with 'I have higher guidance available to me always.'

"So the Punisher now disappears because you're taking your energy away from it—because it's not a real being, although it may have come to think of itself as one. You created it, and therefore you can un-create it. You notice that to divest yourself of the Punisher you had to put into the subconscious the argument, 'I don't need you because I am now aware I have a Higher Self. So you are to merge, you are to go into the light now. You have a bigger job now. The Higher Self will give you that job. Go now.'"

We checked using NMR and found that my Punisher was gone but I still had some inner ages who felt they were bad.

"So," Pamela said, "you can see why it's good to dismantle the Punisher before working with sexual abuse. You can work with those other ages at home. We'll talk about that later. So now I'm going to say a couple of things here: Sexual abuse is a powerful spiritual lesson for all involved. Sexual abuse can be mental and not physical, but even if it's mental, to the child it is the same as physical, it has the same ramifications. The people who are abusers—sometimes it is their body doing it but not them; someone else, another spirit, has come into the body. And very, very often the abuser is in an altered state.

"So sexual abuse is never about making somebody wrong and somebody right. It's about discovering what happened and then finding out how it made the person feel like a victim, how it made them feel powerless, and how they can get that power back. A child, even a baby, has far more power available to it than it realizes, which at the moment bad things are happening is hard to remember. But now you have this older self to help the younger self recognize those things.

"In light of your journey, you want to lift your vibrations. Heavy thoughts, beliefs, and emotions resulting from trauma to this body weigh down the vibrations, and sexual abuse is traumatic. So we need to find the negative thoughts and beliefs and change them so you can lift your emotions and your vibrations.

"So I would ask your Higher Self: 'Is there sexual abuse present, and if so, is there an inner age traumatized by it?' If it isn't present, no need to deal with it. It might have happened, but you've processed it. If it is present, then you need to deal with it. We don't even have to use the real names of the people involved. It's part of your history, part of your body's experience."

More NMR revealed that I still had trauma in my body from the sexual abuse and the memories of it were causing anger and fear. "The clue," Pamela interjected, "why I jumped into this, was the constipation. When a child is extremely constipated on a chronic, long-term basis, it's a huge red flag there could be sexual abuse."

We spent quite a bit of time with NMR to find out what had happened. It turned out that I was sexually abused from age three to age five by my Uncle Tom, my mother's brother. Today it was my three-year-old who came forward. The physical details of the abuses emerged during the regressions.

"And remember, Ann, Uncle Tom could have been in an altered state. More often than not, the abuser was abused and they are acting out their old memories. And memory is an altered state. It's in the subconscious."

We tested and found that yes, Uncle Tom had been in an altered state. Both he and my mother had been abused as children. Now he was the grown-up alone with a child. His old memories came flooding back, putting him into an altered state. He was doing what had been done to him.

"So maybe," Pamela suggested, "this is what the subconscious has been throbbing the arm about: when are you going to get to this? We've been talking about anger, and there is extreme anger here.

"So that the three-year-old hears what would be necessary, we need to regress to her, talk to her about it, and help her release her anger and help her overcome her fear by helping her to stop the abuse. And if her anger wants to lash out at Uncle Tom, she can do so. Because the whole deal is about her finding and regaining her power. And we want to help the body also because it was made to feel powerless as well.

"We teach our children to put up with these things by teaching them, in subtle ways, you're too little, you're too young, you're too weak, and after all, it's Uncle Tom. And there's fear, especially if the molester says, 'If you yell, I'll kill you or I'll hurt your mom, or everyone will think you're bad, or this is a bad thing we're doing, so don't tell.'

"A child's body, anyone's body, has tremendous strength when it's fighting for its life. And yes, a small body can be overcome by a larger body *unless* it allows that spiritual energy to come in which can not only empower the physical body but empower the mind to do things with the molester to weaken him. But the body needs the spiritual essence that's there in order to do this. It has to be given permission to fight for itself when it feels like it gave in and it has all that locked-in anger.

"So we want the child to tell us what happened and be pulled *into* what was happening so we can give the child permission to tell the body to yell, to kick, to hit, to say no. I do often like to make certain they at least verbalize it and get that energy out, and after they do that, to make certain the spirit stays in the body to help give the body that power that it needs to stop the molester.

"We all come in with soul lessons, life lessons. I believe the overriding lesson is, 'When I lose that connection with my spiritual self, can I find my way back to it? In the deepest, darkest places, can I find it?' Being sexually abused as a child is one of the deepest, darkest places you can go because you have all the powerless elements there—powerless because 'I'm too small,' powerless for a girl because 'I'm a girl,' powerless because it's Uncle Tom. And you have this society thing: 'I'm powerless because I'm supposed to be nice.'

"So you let go of your power and your sense of self. And if in that deep, dark place you can re-find that connection and re-find that power, now you've made a huge leap forward. I think it's one of the final tests of power. Can I overcome the stereotype? Can I overcome the society thing? Can I overcome the family thing? Can I overcome the 'I'm a girl' thing? Can I overcome 'this is naughty'? Can I overcome the threat? Can I overcome *all* that, and think, 'No! I will *not* allow you to do this to my body. This I will *not* accept. I will stop you.'

"And then to go further and help the little girl *feel*, by helping her understand it was *not* her fault, she is *not* bad, her body is not bad, and the sex that took place was not healthy sex, it was unhealthy, unnatural sex, and to help her understand *un*healthy, *un*natural sex is not the kind of healthy, natural sex she'll enjoy as an adult. There are all these elements that we want the three-year-old to understand so that she no longer feels powerless or feels shame or anger or bad about herself *or* the memory.

"So in a sense, here's what we're doing: There are dimensions of the mind in which memory exists, and there are images of what happened, and there is energy. When you do a regression, you're going back and reviewing what happened and now you're creating another set of images and energy. So both memories are there. It's kind of like painting a new picture over an old canvas. The old picture is still there, but you paint the new picture over it, and which picture draws your attention depends on which remains more vivid.

"So if you make the new picture—the change, the power, the healing—much more vivid, you put much more belief and energy into it. Now when you think of the memory, *this* is the more glowing picture and you say, 'Yes, that happened to me *but* it was a part of my childhood and I grew from it, I became stronger from it, and so I have no shame of it. Now I understand it.' I'm explaining this so that you—the protector of the three-year-old who will be there too—understand what we're doing. We'll do that in our next session.

"So let's make sure we didn't open the door on anything that's going to make you uncomfortable over the weekend.

We're going to say to the three-year-old self, 'What is a good place where the three-year-old you would love to be over the weekend? Let's create a safe place for you to go. Let's create a place in the mind where you, three-year-old, and *all* of Ann's other children can be together.

"See that house there? That's the girl's house. And in that house there's a big, sunny room full of lots of toys and lots and lots of light. And look, there is Ann's one-year-old and her two-year-old and her four-year-old and her five-year-old. Can you see them? You're all in that room together.

"So let's have all the other children be very solicitous and comforting to the three-year-old, giving a lot of nurturing and loving and protection. And we're going to say there is no way Uncle Tom or his spirit can get at the three-year-old because we are now surrounding the girl's house and the outlying property in a cocoon of white light with gold light all around it, with hawks and eagles and other animals that allow no one in.

"And when it's time to talk to the three-year-old on Monday, I will ask permission to enter or to meet at a neutral place, and we'll make certain it's something she wants to talk about. And I will tell her we will go at her pace. If she doesn't want to remember it, if she just wants to sort of talk about it and not do any of the other stuff, we will go at her pace. But we want her to know you'll be there, adult Ann. And I'll be there, and *most* important of all, her light will be there, because that's her weapon, that's what we're seeking to reconnect her with.

"You can show her beforehand, adult Ann—in fact, here's a little assignment: Meet with her and talk to her about the Higher Self that is the light inside her. The essence of spirit is light, and when I talk to inner children about the Higher Self they relate much better to light inside themselves. And that light can talk to them. And that light can make them strong.

"I say to them, 'There's a boulder there, a great big boulder. Try to move it.' And they say, 'Oh, I can't.' And I say, 'Tell the light inside yourself you want to move the boulder and ask it how you can do that.' And then the light will generally say things like, 'Just do it' or 'Ask to make your body strong and I'll do that,' and then they can usually move the boulder or lift heavy things. So we begin to give them the idea that when they use that light inside them they're very, very strong. So we can use that light. Have her use her light to do something she thinks she can't do. Then she can tell us about it on Monday."

I was surprised to learn that I had been sexually molested as a child. I had absolutely no conscious recollection of it. Yet the more I thought about it, the more I recognized how it had manifested in my relationships. I was eager to find out how to help a molested child heal from the trauma. And I was excited to communicate mentally with my three-year-old over the weekend.

Chapter 9

HEALING SEXUAL ABUSE

I came into today's session ready to learn how to heal abuse. I had no idea what to expect, but clearly it had to be done. My three-year-old needed to take back her power from Uncle Tom.

"The weekend was great," I told Pamela. "My three-year-old and I had a lot of fun. Wait 'til you hear what she did!"

We got right to the induction. ". . . back through time as the form gets smaller and smaller. That's it. Back to age three as the arms are shorter, the legs are shorter, the torso is smaller. And at three—three years old—moving your energy, your awareness into that three-year-old self. I am looking for that three-year-old as she pulls me to where she is waiting— that perfect place to talk. I'm finding you, Ann. Are you there, three-year-old Ann? [No response.] Are we playing hide and seek? [She giggles.] You giggled, and so now I found you! That was a good game! I hear you've been playing games with grown-up Ann all weekend, and she's been showing you how strong your mind is."

"Yeah. I made a teddy bear sit up."

"Wow! That was excellent! How did you do it?"

"I just knew I could tell the teddy bear that if it wanted to play, I needed it to sit up. And it sat up. It was lying down and it sat up! And I made a cat go away."

"You did? How did you do that?"

"Well, this kitty cat was coming toward us, and we pretended like we didn't want it to come toward us, so I said, 'Stop, kitty cat, stop. You can't come toward me. You can't come near me.' And it stopped! It kind of looked at me funny, but it stopped. And I said, 'You stay there. You can't come any closer.' And then I think it got bored and it turned around and walked away."

"And what do you think made that happen?"

"I did. Ann told me I could make things happen that I wanted to make happen, and that I could make things stay away or make things come to me that I want or are good for me."

"You know, that's absolutely true. The trick is to learn to do that in an upsetting situation, when the body feels afraid. When the brain and the body are saying, 'Oh no, oh no,' and they want to hide or run away, or they want to get really, really small and go away—*then* is when you need to know how to use that power."

"Yeah, 'cuz you can *forget*. When you're scared you can forget, huh?"

"Yes, you can. We're going to teach you how *not* to forget, how to use that, how to remember and remind yourself, 'Oh wait a minute. I have *power*. I can use that power. Like with Uncle Tom."

"Hmm."

"Yeah. What happened with Uncle Tom?"

"I don't like Uncle Tom."

"From what I hear about him, I don't like him either."

"He's bad. He hurt me."

"Tell me how he hurt you."

"He stuck things in me and he grabbed me, and I tried to get away but he was too big, and he grabbed me and he squeezed my arm so hard I thought it was gonna fall off. He grabbed it so hard I looked to see if it was still there! And I tried to make him let go, but he was just too strong. I couldn't get his hand off my arm. And nobody was around. Nobody was there. My mom would have made him go away, and my dad would have made him go away, but there was nobody there. I don't understand. How could they leave me with him? He's so *bad*. He's so *mean*."

"Do you think maybe he doesn't show his mean side to them?"

"Oh, no. He's always happy and—well, he's not really happy, though. That's the problem. But no, he doesn't show his mean self."

"He just waits and brings it out when he's all alone with children?"

"Well, me anyway."

"So mommy and daddy didn't realize."

"No."

"Did you try and tell them when they came home what Uncle Tom did?"

"No, 'cuz it was too *bad*."

"How did you know it was bad, Ann?"

[Yells] "'Cuz it *hurt!*"

"But if you hurt your knee or your arm you'd tell them, right?"

"Yeah, but he held on to me and he took some of his clothes off—well, not off, but he unzipped his pants and stuff. And I'd seen one of those things. I mean my dad has one of those things. We see each other naked all the time at home, and my dad has one of those things, but it's not like this. This thing was big and hard.

"First he stuck his finger up me, in the front where I pee. It hurt but it also felt kind of good until he stuck it up too far and then it *hurt*. And I wiggled to get away from him, but I didn't kick him. I should have just kicked him. Then he finally stopped doing that. But that was a piece of cake. Then he took that *thing*, it's this big, hard *thing*, and he put it up next to my mouth and I wouldn't open my mouth. So he grabbed my cheeks and made me open my mouth and he stuck it in my mouth. And it was salty. It was like ugh! Yuck!

"I thought that was pretty disgusting. But then he actually turned me over and pulled my bottom apart with his hands and he tried to stick it in *there*. That *hurt*. It was like, 'It's too *big*, it's too *big*.' And I don't know, I didn't feel anything after that. I think I just stopped feeling anything. I just wanted it to stop. I just wanted it to go away. I wanted *him* to go away. And my arm hurt so bad. Oh, he's so horrible. He's so disgusting. Why? Why did he do that? I don't think you're supposed to do that. I don't think big people are supposed to do that to little people. It's not fair."

"It isn't fair," Pamela echoed. "It's not fair at all. I'm so sorry that you had to discover that there are these kinds of people in the world. He's sick in his head. He's a sick person in his head. This isn't healthy and this isn't good and this isn't what big people are supposed to do to children, or what children are supposed to do to children.

"Your Uncle Tom is not nice. And this not-nice part of him, you and your body need to protect yourself from Uncle Tom. I know you tried to yell, but nobody was there, right?"

"Well I really didn't try to yell-yell. I just kept trying to kick him and wiggle and get away from him and stuff. But he's so *big*."

"Yeah. So you're going to have to use your *mind* too, Ann, to help your body be really, really strong. Your mind is going to be part of this. So let's go back to when he first grabs your arm. I bet that made your arm really, really mad."

"Oh yeah."

"I know it made the whole body mad. But I bet it made the arm maddest of all. So, when he grabs your arm, stare at him really hard and say *no* so you really mean it. Let him know in your mind, 'I'll hurt you if you don't let go of my arm.' But he's the kind of guy who probably won't listen. You'll probably have to prove it, huh? Besides, your arm is *mad*. You warned him.

"So now with your mind you're going to do two things at once that will make him *really* weak. He's big, but you can drain him of his energy and make him *really* weak and you can make your arm *really* strong—both your arms and your legs. And your *strong* arm that he grabbed, make it all *hot* so it burns his hands [she giggles] and jerk that arm away. What does your angry arm want to do?"

"You mean when . . . I don't understand."

"Does your arm want to show him how that hurt? Would your angry arm like to grab his arm and pinch it?"

"No. I don't care about that. I just want to show him that he can't grab me, that he can't do those things to me. And if he tries to grab me, I'm makin' my arm so hot that I'll burn his fingers."

"That's right! How does he look when you let him know that?"

"Really surprised!"

"So let's go to when he puts his finger in your—vagina first, didn't he?"

"Uh-huh."

"Okay. At first it felt sort of good, right?"

"Uh-huh."

"Okay. That's true. The vagina has *feelings* that when something feels good it goes, 'Okay, that feels good.' But he went too far, which made your vagina mad. And I think you said you wanted to kick."

"Uh-huh."

"So why don't you let the vagina *push* his finger out and let his finger know, 'No, I don't like you in me.' So let it *sting* him and push the finger out, and let your legs kick him really hard, Ann."

"Okay. Oooh, I've got all these muscles in there and they can just like squeeze on it and push it back out."

"Very good! That's a good, strong, powerful vagina. It knows how to protect itself. And now, the legs get all strong and powerful and they know exactly how to kick and where to kick...."

"Oh, I wish my legs were just a little bit longer 'cuz then I could kick that big old thing. But my legs are too short. I know! I'll make my legs grow a little."

"There you go!"

"I'll make my legs grow, and then I can give him a good kick right there between his legs. Ooh, he's bending over. Ooh, that was really good 'cuz that *hurt* him!"

"That's a good signal," Pamela exclaimed. "People who are sick in the mind like he is, they don't like to get hurt. That's why they pick on little children, because they think the child will think they're too little. Well, you're showing him a little child has a lot of power."

"Yeah!"

"When the child puts that body and mind together, they have tremendous power. So you've let him know that. Your body is letting him know, 'No! No, you can't! You won't. I won't let you hurt me.' Now I know he also pinched your cheeks, which means your cheeks are mad. And putting that thing in your mouth made your mouth mad. So what do your cheeks, your tongue, and your mouth want to do?"

"I'll put points on my teeth and I'll bite it!"

"There you go. Feel that. You bite it, and he yelps and yells, and then you blow him away. Blow him right across the room. Or blow him outdoors. Just show him how powerful you are. He looks mighty surprised!"

"And silly!"

"And silly," Pamela echoed.

"Yeah, he's so surprised. He looks so silly! He looks stupid!"

"He *is* stupid. Okay. So now let your bottom show its power and anger, too. When he poked that in, that made your bottom really mad. So you'd better let your bottom protect itself too. You have powerful muscles there, too, you know."

"Yeah. I can just close 'em up and not let him in."

"That's right! And I'll bet you can kick backwards, too!"

"Yeah. I'll figure out a way I can just give him a good kick."

"Okay, Ann, you need to find out what you need to do with your body to get him off you. How does your body need to move, and what do you need to do with your mind to make that happen? You search around and...."

"This is a hard one. If I stick my rear end *up* that's not gonna be good 'cuz that just might make it go in more. So I've gotta think about this."

"Well, you closed it off. But you can use it now as a weapon. I bet it would like that! You can...."

"I've got it! I'll roll over and kick him again and make him hurt and bend over and hold that thing, and he's saying it really hurts. And he looks so silly!"

"So now your legs are feeling very powerful, your teeth, your mouth, your cheeks are feeling very powerful, your bottom, your vagina. What about those arms? They need to feel powerful, too. What do the *arms* want to do?"

"Well, my arm just wants to rest 'cuz that was bad, and when I made it really hot, it's just like kinda cooling down right now."

"Why don't you use your mind to *really* heal that arm? Right now, heal that arm and use that arm now to tie him up, maybe. That arm needs to feel its power, and we can't leave it feeling it's a victim. It got hot like it was supposed to, but we also want it to feel that it's strong and powerful. Whether it wants to hit him, or whether it wants to point at him and say 'never again' or whether it wants to show him your muscles—but that arm, we need to unlock the anger in it. Let's make *certain* that that anger is gone."

"Well, when I kicked him, he's bent down in the corner hanging on to his thing 'cuz he's hurt so bad. So I'm going to take my arm and make a fist and I'm beatin' him up on the shoulders and I'm beatin' him up on the head. He's all crouched over and I'm just beatin' him up."

"Very good. Getting all that anger out, you just do it 'til it's all gone, that anger. And then you tell him what you think of him, Ann. And you tell him that never, *ever* will he hurt you again."

"Yeah. I think you're mean and you're sick and why don't you pick on somebody your own size? Ugh, you're a creepy old man. And you can't hurt me anymore. Because you see? I can hurt *you*. I made *you* hurt, but you can't make *me* hurt. So you stay away from me. And you stay away from all the other little kids too 'cuz I'll tell you something. All the other little kids can do the same thing I just did to you. So go find somebody your own size and try . . . don't even try it on them.

"What's the matter with you? You'd better be careful or they're going to cut that thing off. But you're not hurting me *any more*. I'll use my arms and I'll use my teeth and I'll use my feet, all my muscles—I'll use everything I've got so that you can't hurt me any more.

"You're a mean old man. And I don't want any of those stupid dolls you bring me either. That just makes everybody think that you're nice. And you're not nice. So just *stay away* from me. You can't hurt me *any more*. And you stay away from *all* kids. You can't hurt them, either. Just go be mean somewhere else—although it'd be nice if you weren't mean. But if you gotta be mean, be mean somewhere else."

"Well done, Ann! That was powerful! And that was strong! And what are you going to tell mommy and daddy when they get home? Why don't you tell them he's not to stay with you anymore."

"Yeah. I'll tell them that I don't want to stay with Uncle Tom *any more* and he's not nice and he just bit off a little more than he could chew with me."

"Excellent! How are they reacting to that, Ann?"

"They're shocked. But they believe me."

"Yes! That's really good."

"I think he needs a wife—to do all that stuff to. I mean she may want it, but not little kids."

"Well put, Ann. You did really well and. . . ."

"Oh wait a minute. I just gotta give him a black eye. I gotta use my arm. I wanna give him a black eye. Just punch him, just—pow—and give him a big black eye. 'Cuz then . . . see, right now nobody is ever gonna know. But if he's got a black eye, people are gonna ask him where he got the black eye and he's gonna have to think up some really stupid story of where he got that black eye. And I'm gonna tell mom and dad that *I* gave him that black eye."

"That is very smart of you, Ann. Now tell me, are there any other times with Uncle Tom that you want to talk about right now?"

"Well, I really don't remember. I know that he does it lots of times. But I'll just do all the same things to him again that I did this time and he won't be able to hurt me again. So bring him on!"

"Well done, three-year-old. Very good! Where do you want to go now? Would you like to go back to the little girl's house?"

"Yeah. I love it there!"

"Okay. That place of light—see that light, Ann, and move right into it, into that joy, that playful joy, as the three-year-old moves right into that playful, joyful place."

"It's fun now because now I don't have to be afraid of grown-ups. I mean, I don't have to be afraid of all the men grown-ups that they might do that to me. Before, I was always a little suspicious of . . . were they going to do something, were they going to hurt me? But now I know that—hah, let 'em try. They'll be sorry.

"But I really don't have to worry about it 'cuz I know I'm strong enough. They'll just know. They'll just see it. They'll think, 'Uh-oh, I shouldn't mess with her 'cuz she's too strong. I'm gonna be sorry if I mess with her.' So I don't really even have to think about it.

"And someday I'll be able to tell other little girls that they can have power too, and that they don't have to put up with that nonsense. But I guess for now I've just gotta be happy that *I* know it. It's making things a whole lot nicer for me, that's for sure. I can be happy and skip around and not walk around all the time with my fists clenched. I can *relax*. That's the thing I can do. I can let all those muscles relax and not have to squeeze to keep people out. And my arm—now it's a weapon instead of a victim."

"Good. *Very* good. That's a wonderful realization. Okay, so the three-year-old goes into her place and the body is feeling very empowered as you focus on your breathing, the body feeling very strong, the body feeling important, the body feeling powerful, the body *using* that power for healing.

"And as you also, adult Ann, focus on opening up to that universal healing energy—light—you can feel that light coming in through the crown chakra, and as you direct it with your thoughts into your arm, you feel that healing energy. And you focus for a moment on the right arm, filling the right arm with healing light, that healing energy. So on those energy levels that right arm is now moving into its perfection. All bruising disappears. Any damage disappears as on the energy levels that arm is restored to its perfect condition.

"It happens as quickly as thought on the energy levels. In the physical levels we also have the element of time, and that slows it down a little bit. But right now you have transcended time. You can actually transfer that healing right into the physical arm, and if the cells are willing to accept it right now, they will. But if they want to do it at a more slow and steady pace, that will happen. At any rate, your arm is now in that healing mode, and with every breath it's filled with light instead of anger. It feels so good.

"And at one, hypnosis is over...."

"That was pretty incredible," I exclaimed. "And she was so inventive! I loved her putting points on her teeth. And the black eye so people would ask where he got it—that was great!

"So this is how you deal with abuse. I can see how conscious mind therapy wouldn't heal all the emotions. We had to go to my three-year-old, to that level of consciousness where it all happened, and help her *feel* her power. It's another example of create-uncreate, isn't it? We had to go to where the anger and shame and guilt and fear were created in order to un-create it and replace it with power."

"Exactly, Ann. Well put," Pamela replied.

"If abuse is one of the big lessons—learning to reconnect with your light in the dark place of abuse—how often do you think it happens? You mentioned once that excess weight is often a signal of unresolved abuse. If that's the case, my guess would be the answer is pretty often."

"It's huge," Pamela responded, "way up there in the high percentiles."

"Yet I had absolutely no conscious recollection of my abuse at all, although I must say I never did like Uncle Tom. I just never knew why."

Healing my abused three-year-old wasn't a dark, ominous experience at all. It was fascinating and exhilarating and often amusing. She was so clever! My arm had stopped throbbing as soon as my three-year-old started talking during hypnosis. What a great signal she had used! She had made my right arm hurt exactly where Uncle Tom had made hers hurt.

CHAPTER 10

WASHING IT ALL AWAY

After the session in which my three-year-old discovered her power, I thought she was at peace, but she wasn't finished. She used my arm again to signal me. I was learning that healing complex issues often takes several sessions.

My arm had felt perfect for two days. But it started throbbing again the next time I was on my way to see Pamela. We started the session with NMR and learned that my three-year-old had more to talk about. Once I was in hypnosis, we found her in the girl's house, and she was glad to see us. Pamela asked her to go back to that place with Uncle Tom.

"Where is everybody?" she asked. "Nobody's here to *help* me. Nobody's *here*. There's always somebody around. But now when I really need them, nobody's here."

"Is Uncle Tom saying anything to you, Ann?"

"I don't hear him say anything except, 'Be quiet, just be quiet. This is you-and-me time,' he says. I don't *want* you-and-me time. I don't *like* it. *It hurts* me. He says, 'This is you-and-me time and only you and I know about this, and if you tell anybody else about this I'll hurt you more.' So now I don't know what to do. If I don't tell anybody then nobody can help me. But if I tell anybody he'll hurt me more. Somebody's got to help me. What'd I do? I must have *done* something to make him think he can do this to me." [She starts to cry.]

"You know, Ann," Pamela explained, "you didn't do anything. Your Uncle Tom—I'm going to tell you a big word for a little girl to hear—is what we call a pedophile. Do you know what that means? That means an adult person who has a sickness in their head and they like to hurt children like this. They hurt any child they can get alone like this.

"So you and I need to help you know how you can handle this because pedophiles like your Uncle Tom are very sneaky and very good at getting children all alone. They know how to tell children's parents things that reassure the parents and make the parents feel their child will be safe with this person. They're very clever and sneaky at that. They know how to say things in a way and act in a way that the adult people believe them.

"But first I want to say to you, Ann, it was very, *very* smart of you to tell somebody, to tell me. It was very smart because that takes away the pedophile's power. They act in secret. And because they tell children they'll hurt them more, that's real scary.

"Your body already feels very hurt, doesn't it? So if they say they'll hurt you more, then you aren't going to tell and that's what the pedophile is afraid of. He's afraid of the child telling because he knows the other adults will say, 'You're doing bad things. That is sick. We are going to lock you up and see if we can fix you.' And that's what he doesn't want. So telling was very, very smart.

"And the second thing to learn here, Ann, is what to do when there's nobody around to help you. That's a very, very important thing to learn. Because there *is* help when there's nobody around to help you. There is help from the invisible world. Do you know about that world? Did you see it when you were littler?"

"No."

"I'll bet if you close your eyes . . . now let's walk away from Uncle Tom for a moment. Let's lock him up. He's a pedophile. You *push* him into that little cage over there until we're ready to deal with him, okay? Push him into the cage and lock it real fast and tell him, 'I *will* tell, I *have* told, and you won't hurt me *any* more. I'll be back and you'll be sorry!' [My three-year-old stops crying and giggles at the idea of locking up Uncle Tom.]

"So let's walk away from Uncle Tom for a minute because you and I need to talk about this invisible world because that's the one you need to call on. I'll bet when you were *very* little—and I'll bet if you think about it for a moment, you'll remember when you were one or two—there were people you saw that your mommy and daddy didn't see. Maybe children. Maybe even fairies. Sometimes people call these invisible people spirits, some people call them souls, some people call them ghosts. But they aren't ghosts. Ghosts are the ones that try to scare you. But we're not even going to talk about them because you have the power to keep them away. That's why I want to talk to you about the invisible world.

"The invisible world is always there. And there are always people to help. And the most important one who comes to help is your own powerful, invisible self. There is around you an invisible self. It's bigger than your body and it's very, very powerful. And it shines really bright, which is why I sometimes call it your light. To the adult Ann I talk about Higher Self, but it's the same thing. It's your *light*. It's your light self. It's your *powerful* self. It's the part that can help you. It's doing it right now.

"You said, 'Somebody needs to help me,' and here's your light self and here I am, and then there's the adult Ann, too, all present wanting to help. You have help all around you. And our job is to help you know how strong and powerful you can be when you use your mind as well as your body.

"The mind can do amazing things—like, three-year-old, put your arm out beside you. That's it. And focus on that arm and tell that arm in your mind that it's getting really light— that all that light around you is lifting up that arm. And that you can feel that light just coming inside that arm. It's filling every bone, making the bones lighter. It's filling every muscle, making the muscles lighter. It's filling the skin, making the skin lighter and the thumbs and the fingers lighter, as light as a feather. And as you focus on that arm lifting up, just stare at the arm in your mind and think, 'Rise up. Lift up. Float up. Float in the air.'

"I bet you begin to notice that arm starting to want to float. And the more you tell it to float, the more that arm listens to you and begins to float. It's like it has light inside and gets lighter and lighter, floating that arm up, lifting that arm up higher and higher. Just floating up. Floating up! There you go! [My arm lifts off the armrest.]

"That arm is responding to your thoughts! That arm is listening to you. You're doing that with your mind. Now tell the arm, 'Oh, that feels so good!' And as you float, all that light inside you feels so good. Now you can tell the arm, 'Okay, you can rest now. Go down and rest.'

"And you're going to bring all that light not only in your arm but in your whole body, three-year-old Ann, and you're going to wash away *all* that shame and guilt, *all* that ugly stuff that your uncle put on you. You're going to tell that light, 'Wash my body inside and outside. Get it all sparkly clean before I go deal with Uncle Tom. I'm going to do it with a sparkly clean body so he understands he didn't leave a mark on me, so he can see he didn't get to me, he didn't leave his ugly touch on me at all.'

"So you're using all that light to just wash yourself inside and outside. Wash your mouth, wash your bottom, wash your back and your arm and your chest and your hips and your thighs. That's it—washing every single part of yourself, washing it so good. That's it.

"Now, the body wants to say to you, 'Ann, that power in your mind, you could tell a rock to float and if you had enough faith in your mind to do that and if the light around you said, 'Oh, that would be a good thing to do right now,' you could do that. But more important, you can use that power inside your mind to lock your uncle up even without a cage. You can use that power inside your mind to paralyze him so that his arms can't move and his legs can't move and he can't move at all. And then you can push him and you can get him off you and away from you and you can tell him what you think of him and you can have total power over him.

"That would be very scary to him. Then he would know what it felt like to you. You can use your mind—and you're going to *have* to use your mind, Ann, because when we go back to remembering what he did and how your body felt like it was being pinned down and couldn't move, and it cried out, 'Somebody help me!' then you're going to say, 'Hey! You're *my* body. *I'll* help you. I'm going to use *my* spirit, *my* light, *my* mind, and I'm going to help you help yourself, body. Together we're going to do it. I'll paralyze him and then you push him away.' That's what you're going to say to your body, right? Are you ready to do that?"

"Uh-huh."

"Do you feel ready to do that? Have you got your mind all ready for that? Okay. Then, be very brave and be right back in that moment when you feel the weight of his body and you feel him grabbing and holding your arms, and you said you can't even wiggle, you can't move. And your body is saying, 'Help me, help me!' Talk to your body in your mind. Say, 'You're my body. I'll help you.'"

"You're my body. I'll help you. We're going to turn this guy into a statue."

"There you go. You paralyze him right now in your mind. You just see him turning to stone. And he can't move his arms, and he can't move his legs."

"He can't move anything. He can't even blink!"

"Boy! What do you see in his eyes?" Pamela asks.

"Nothing, 'cuz they're stone now. Well, surprise! He's really surprised." [She laughs.]

"So you take that stone statue body and you get it off of you. If you need to levitate a little to do that, you can do that with your mind, but you and your body, your mind and body work together and you get him *off you*. And maybe you want to lift him up with your mind, tell him what you think of him, this old pedophile. You might tell him you know what he *is*."

"'I know what you are, and I know you're a bad man, and I'm going to kick you and you're going to turn into a pile of dust! So this will teach you to mess with little kids, especially with me!' Then I pull both knees back and I give him a good push with both my legs and he goes flying across the room and he hits the wall. And when he hits the wall he breaks [she laughs an even bigger laugh], and he just smashes and I look down and there's this pile of little rocks that used to be the statue. He's gone. He's not going to hurt me again and he's not going to hurt any other little kids again. Because I took care of myself but I also helped all the other kids that he would have gotten."

"Yes, you did! That was a very good, powerful, strong thing to do. I'm so glad, Ann, that you told him, *'You're* the bad one.' You were right. It's not you. You didn't do anything bad, you didn't do anything wrong. And your mind knew what he was doing was wrong. You were listening to it. Now is there any part of his body that your body is mad at and wants to do or say anything to?"

"It's more his mind that I'm really mad at. 'You stupid old . . . who do you think you are to take little kids that don't *think* they can defend themselves? You get to them before they know they can defend themselves. You get 'em when they're really little and they think all they can do is just let you do whatever you want to do.

"Now I know that I don't have to worry about being hurt. I know that I can just fill myself up and make whatever I want happen to whoever's trying to hurt me. So actually, thanks a lot, Uncle Tom. You showed me the power that I have, and I might not ever have known this if it weren't for you. So, in a way, thanks for being a sicko dirty old man and showing me the powers that I have to protect myself."

"Very, very good. I'm really proud of you, three-year-old. You listened to your mind that told you this wasn't right, and even though he said you shouldn't tell anyone, you did, and that helped you find that power inside you, so you don't ever, ever have to be afraid of being alone, *ever*. Now I want you to scan your body, three-year-old, and tell me if your mouth is feeling clean and relaxed and perfect."

"It feels relaxed. But it doesn't really feel clean."

"I want you to turn around because somebody very special has come for you. There's an angel there, three-year-old. And there's a very special spring of holy water that the angel guards. That's her job. And she went to that spring of holy water and she got water for you. That's how special you are. She brought you the holy water to drink in your mouth that's going to wash away all that energy of your Uncle Tom. So as you put it to your lips those lips feel blessed by that holy water, and as it goes on your tongue and throughout your mouth and down your throat, that holy water brings complete and perfect healing. There we go. That's it. Good. Very good.

"And now she has another cup of holy water and she says, 'Here, let me help you wash your bottom. And the angel pours the holy water in your bottom where you go poop and that water seeps in. And she pours the water on your back and on your vagina and on your legs, and she pours the holy water on your arms. She's blessing your body. Can you imagine—an angel here for *you*, blessing *your* body with holy water. They don't do that for bad people, do they? Only for the very, very best of children. That's you. That angel with holy water is helping you cleanse your body totally and completely, washing away all those remnants you have of shame or fear or guilt or anger—just washing away. . . .'"

"I need some right here on my arm." [She points to where he grabbed her.]

"Well, tell the angel you need some right here."

"Angel, I need some right here. This hurts."

"Oh, not only is she putting water on it. She's kissing it and folding her angel wings right around the arm and blessing it, bringing in that healing touch, that healing energy. I bet that arm feels loved—kissed by an angel. That spot on your arm will always feel special; it will always feel blessed. It's been kissed by an angel. How special that is. How beautiful that is. So perfect, so wonderful!

"And now the angel is holding you and saying, 'Sleep now, my child. Sleep now.' Sleep enfolded in God's love. Sleep surrounded with light. And move deep into that healing place where all the cells of the body repair and move right into that perfect balance.

"And now the adult Ann too is feeling that presence of your light surrounding you. And the subconscious, that subconscious servant, is aware of this healing light and is using it to restore the body, to heal the body, to move the body into the levels of perfect form and energy.

"And now on that screen of the mind you see being erased: 'If I tell, I will be hurt.' Erasing: 'I'm afraid to tell. It's scary to tell. I can't tell.' Erasing: 'There is no one to help me, I'm all alone.' Erasing: 'I must have done something wrong. I must be bad.' And erasing: 'I'm too little, too weak, too powerless.' Erasing: 'My body isn't strong enough.' And erasing: 'My mommy and daddy don't care—they left me alone with a bad man.' Getting that whole screen completely blank.

"And now telling the programmer to remove these and replace them with: 'I am loved. I am strong. I am powerful. I am never alone. My mind is masterful. My body is powerful. My spirit is light, and light is the greatest power of all. My mind and my body and my spirit have mastery over matter. I can protect myself. I do protect myself. I am good. I'm a good child and a good adult. Spirit loves to be with my body. I am a good body. I am important, my body. I love my body. I know my body loves me.'

"And you are feeling so content, thinking, 'Yes, mind is so powerful.' And higher consciousness always has power over lower consciousness. Pedophiles are very stuck in a lower consciousness and are very susceptible to the power of suggestion. It is a very powerful tool with the lower consciousness of all people. And it's a very powerful tool for the body, too."

"With the thought, 'Feeling empowered, feeling cleansed, feeling special, feeling blessed . . . ,' hypnosis is over," Pamela concluded the regression.

After the regression we did some NMR, which confirmed that my three-year-old no longer felt anger, shame, guilt, or fear.

"That was great!" I exclaimed. "But I thought my three-year-old was feeling okay after we talked to her last time. Why did she come up again?"

"The level of the three-year-old today was still upset that no one was there to help her. That's why I told her about pedophiles and how sneaky they are and why I told her about the invisible world."

"Yeah, I think she really took that to heart. I had all those invisible friends later on, remember? Is it ever possible for someone to heal an abused inner age themselves?"

"Those that have had a lot of emotional trauma can't. They're just going to have too much inner resistance. But they can do some things on their own to get to a place where they make their healing a priority."

"Well," I admitted, "I certainly have a whole new respect for my body! And when I think back on how badly I treated it over the years, I have to apologize to it. 'I'm sorry for treating you so badly, body, and I know the part you play now, and I promise to treat you much, much better.'"

"You know, Ann, most people treat their cars better than they do their bodies."

"I know, when I worked with those dance companies we all lived on sugar. I'm amazed my poor body survived. At least now I eat right. I have to start telling it how much I appreciate it and how grateful I am it survived all my abuse. After all, I am asking it to heal my heart and my toenail, and my eyes. I'd better start giving back."

Since this regression I have, in fact, developed a relationship with my body. I talk to it many times a day. I thank it for staying healthy. I thank it for turning everything I eat to energy. When I put on lotion I thank my skin for staying tight and looking young. I see my body as my partner now. It houses my soul and the emotional part of myself. I owe this new relationship with my body to my three-year-old.

Chapter 11

Telling Mom

My three-year-old was still not completely healed. Children have to hear things many times before they absorb them, and my three-year-old was no different. Although she had told her parents about Uncle Tom before, what happened was still on her mind as a secret.

"Well, Pamela, the exact same thing happened again. My arm felt great until the drive down here today. Do you think it's my three-year-old? Do you think there's more?"

There was. My three-year-old wanted to tell mom about Uncle Tom.

"But she told before. Why does she have to do it again?" I asked.

"Yes, we had her tell mom before," Pamela answered, "but we didn't really let her have the experience. She needs to say the words and have the actual experience. Sometimes what we did the first time would have been enough. But obviously it wasn't enough for her.

"It's very hard for children to keep secrets. They have to wall it off from themselves so they don't know what happened and therefore can't tell what happened. So you start to get a lot more separation of the mind. You have a pocket of information—a memory, an experience—that the subconscious wants you to process because it knows that secrets you keep from yourself make you sick."

Clearly, it was time to talk to my three-year-old about secrets. Once I was in hypnosis, we found her in the girl's house again. She was waiting for us.

". . . And so, three-year-old, we shift our attention to you. I want you to listen first, very carefully. The goal is not to please me or your mother or your father or anyone else. The goal for you is to be truly, truly in joy, in happiness, to be truly your happy, joyful self. Because when you are, you will feel that love, that love of spirit and God for you, that love that can never be taken away. Our job, yours and mine, is to have you talk about thoughts and feelings that keep you from that love, that keep you from feeling it.

"You know, three-year-old, when I was three I had a lot of ugly thoughts. I had mad feelings and sad feelings that I had to talk about. When I did, ah, it was such a release. Something is on your mind. Something seems to be—what would you say—bothering you, distressing you, upsetting you. What is on your mind?"

"Well, Uncle Tom keeps coming back," my three-year-old voice replied. "He flies airplanes and so he's gone most of the time. But then everybody gets all excited because Uncle Tom's coming home. But I'm like, 'Oh no, not *him*. He's going to hurt me.' And I dread it and I just live in this fear.

"*I'm* not excited and *I'm* not happy. But he said he'd hurt me if I told anyone or said anything. So I've got to just be quiet. I don't know if I'm makin' him do it—I don't know anything about that. But I just know that everybody's all excited because he's coming home.

"And he always comes with all these presents for everybody from all these weird places. But *I* know he's going to get me alone and hurt me again. And I *dread* it. I just dread when he's coming. And it's just like, 'Oh gosh, it's next week' and then it's this week and then it's the day after tomorrow and then it's tomorrow, and then I *really* start to get scared and nervous.

"And then we have to go see him. We have to drive all the way to my grandmother's town and go see Uncle Tom, who everybody thinks is so great. He laughs and he smiles like he's a movie star or something. But *I* know he's *terrible,* and I don't want to go and I don't want to see him and I have to listen to all these people talk about how great he is and how wonderful he is. And he's *not*. And I don't know who to tell."

"Why do you think, three-year-old—think about it, I know you're very smart—why do you think he warned you not to tell?"

"'Cuz what he's doing is bad, and they won't like him any more. They'll know he's mean like I know he's mean."

"That's right. So then, doesn't it make sense to tell?"

"Yeah."

"Then I think it's possibly time you told your mommy and daddy. You tell them *exactly* what he does to you. Is that a scary thought?"

"No, actually. [She laughs.] It's going to be fun! I know *exactly* what I'll say."

"Are you going to tell mom first or are you going to tell them both together?"

"Oh, I'll tell mom 'cuz he's *her* brother."

"Where are you going to find mom? Go find her now."

"Okay. She's always in the kitchen. I'll just go into the kitchen. And I'll say, 'Mom, I'm not going to grandma's tomorrow. I don't want to see Uncle Tom. Why don't I want to see him? I'll tell you why. Let me tell you what he does to me.

"Every time I see him and he gets me alone he grabs me, he puts me down on a table or a bed or wherever we are, and then he puts his hands all over me and then he sticks his *thing* in my mouth and then he sticks his finger where I pee and he sticks his *thing* where I poop and he holds me down and then he shivers and shakes and then he stops. And he's got this look on his face—it's like a Halloween mask when he does it. And I don't want to go see him, I don't want to be alone with him.

"Don't you ever, ever, ever leave me alone with him again. He's mean and horrible, and what he's doing is not right. And I'm not going. You can get a babysitter or you or dad can not go and stay here with me. But I am *not* going to grandma's because I don't want any chance of me being alone with Uncle Tom."

"And how does mommy look?"

"She starts to cry. Her face goes white and she says, 'Ann, he really has done all this to you?' And I say, 'Yeah, more than once. Over and over, and every time I see him I know it's going to happen again. And I don't like it and I don't think *you* should like it. And he's *your* brother so you do what you want. But just keep me away from him. I don't ever, ever, ever want to be alone with him again—ever, ever, ever. And I don't want his dolls and I don't want his stuff that he brings me. It just reminds me of this horrible, mean man that did all these things to me."

"The fact that her face went white tells you she believes you, Ann."

"Oh, yeah! She believes me."

"Good. It was good of you to tell. You see, Uncle Tom frightened you and he frightened your body and he made you and your body think if you told, something horrible would happen. So we're going to tell your arm now, something horrible didn't happen. Something wonderful happened. Mom is going to protect you now. Mom's not going to take you to see Uncle Tom. Do you think mom will talk to dad?"

"Oh yeah!"

"What do you think will happen then?"

"I don't know. I think they should put him in jail. [She giggles.] But I don't know. I mean, the whole family—it's going to be big because when Uncle Jim [mom's other brother] has kids he'll probably go after them. And if I get any brothers or sisters he'll probably go after *them*. So this is not good."

"No it isn't. And you're right. Uncle Tom has a problem, and the family needs to know about it because Uncle Tom's problem affects them."

"Yeah."

"And then the family can insist he get help and that might mean he does indeed have to go to jail."

"I don't think they'll make him go to jail. I think as long as he gets help they'll say, 'Okay, you either go to jail or you get help.' Well, I don't know—yeah, mommy would say that. Yeah, she'd probably say, 'Okay, you've got two choices here: jail or help.'"

"But no little girl of mine will be with you," Pamela added.

"Right."

"That was really, really, really good, Ann. You did really good for yourself."

"My mother is thinking, 'Should I tell *my* mother?' That's going to be tough. I don't know what she's going to do about that one. But that's not my problem. All I care about is that they don't leave me alone with him any more and they know why."

"And you took care of that."

"Right."

"You also learned, Ann, that those people that the world judges to be great, sometimes the world doesn't know really what is and what isn't great. You knew who this man *really* was, and you stood up for your truth. That's really important."

"And I know that *I'm* great and he was making me feel that I'm *not* great. And that's a really bad thing to do to people—to make them feel not great."

"Yes it is. And I think that you're going to realize right now that you're not ever, ever going to let anybody make you think that. Because you can see, you can feel, you know how great you are. And you know how powerful your truth is. See how powerful the truth is, Ann? You spoke the truth, and it went right through to mommy and it affected her. She knew you were speaking truth, and she didn't deny it. That's good. She cares about you. You matter to your mommy. And you matter to your daddy. And your body matters to you, and I think your body realizes that. It feels good about that. It stood up for you, and you stood up for it. You and your body make a very, very powerful team."

"Yeah. And she's on the phone calling daddy, and she's saying that he needs to come home right now. She's really upset."

"Of course. It's *that* important. Good for mom, that it's that important that they take care of . . . what are they going to do? Daddy arrives home and how do they take care of their little girl?"

"Well, she talks to him a minute or two, and then we all sit on the couch together and she's rubbing my back. And they're just holding me and telling me that they love me and they'll never leave me alone again with Uncle Tom and it won't ever happen again and they're going to make sure he doesn't do it to any other little girls or boys, too."

"See? They don't think you're bad or naughty, do they?"

"No. They feel really bad because they said I didn't do anything wrong, that it wasn't my fault. He just took advantage of someone littler than him and that sometimes you call those people bullies, when you pick on people that are littler than you."

"Yes. And that's what Uncle Tom is. He is a bully."

"Uh-huh."

"Well good for mom and dad. They really care about you."

"They're *so* mad, though. They're trying not to show it. But they are mad. My mother's figuring out what to do and how to do it, but ooh, they are mad, mad, mad."

"Yup. They're really mad at *him*, not you. Good for you. You really took care of that. They're very proud of you too. So am I. You didn't let those threats stop you. You didn't let the lies hold back your truth. And you didn't let what the world thought of him hold you back either."

"Yeah, 'cuz I knew what the world thought was a lie."

"That's right. And that will serve you well all your life. Well, are you feeling much lighter now, three-year-old?"

"Yeah. I feel much better."

After ending the hypnosis Pamela remarked, "How interesting it is that you and I might have said we think the three-year-old is done, but the higher awareness was, 'No, we need to tell.'"

"So telling before wasn't enough," I commented, "because she hadn't really focused on it. And look what she learned this time about speaking her truth and not buying into the opinions of others.

"This process of regression therapy is fascinating. First I had to take back my power from the abuse and get rid of the shame and guilt. Then I had to tell somebody to get rid of the secret. I would think that would be a pretty universal process, whether you do it in one shot or it takes you three times or whatever."

Pamela explained that good regression therapy involves six steps and there is no telling how many sessions it will take to move through them. Sometimes it can be done in one session, and sometimes it takes more. The six steps, or six R's, are: (1) recognize the origin of the problem with NMR; (2) relive the experience creating the problem; (3) release the negative emotions, thoughts, beliefs creating the problem; (4) re-pattern the experience with empowering actions, emotions, thoughts, and beliefs; (5) realize the lesson and the growth gained; and (6) retest for acceptance and change with NMR.

With further NMR we learned that my three-year-old was no longer in distress. She had taken back her power, released the shame and guilt, and told her secret. The consciousness of my three-year-old was now in the light.

It took only three regressions to heal my three-year-old of her abuse. Compared with other therapy methods, this seemed amazingly fast. This isn't to say healing always happens this fast. Many factors are involved in determining how many sessions complete healing will take. I knew I was working with a skilled therapist, and clearly the key was to regress to the original experience and address the negative thoughts and beliefs one by one so my inner age could take back her power.

CHAPTER 12

HEALING MY OTHER AGES OF ABUSE

I knew my four-year-old and five-year-old would also need help healing from sexual abuse. I wondered which one of them would show up next. I was eager to hear what they had to say because now I knew how to help them heal. In this regression both of them come forward.

"Now my arm is so itchy I want to rip it off," I said as I settled into The Chair. "The signal is different, but do you think it's another age that wants to talk about Uncle Tom?" With NMR we learned this signal was from my five-year-old.

"This is a good example of how when you heal one age, you don't heal them all," Pamela explained. "Each level of your consciousness is unique and complete. So however the three-year-old processed the abuse, now the five-year-old needs to process it for herself. You can also look at it another way: The anger isn't completely dissipated, so now we go to where it's at the five-year-old level. We have to let her release her anger. So let's go talk to her.

"... What comes forward now is five-year-old Ann. Hello, five-year-old. We really, really, *really* want to talk to you today. And we want *you* to talk today because I know bad things happened to you that caused you, of course, to feel upset—probably mad. I know it had to do with Uncle Tom, right?"

"Yeah. You know I'm always very good. I have to be. But I'm not really good in my head 'cuz of this Uncle Tom thing. I mean, I think about it. As I get older he's not around very much, but I think about it all the time and it's like it's happening all over again. I just want it all to go away. I am so *over* this. [She's standing with her hand on her hip as if she's forty.] I am so over this guy! No matter what I do, it creeps in and I'll think about it. I just never quite get rid of it. I mean, it goes away for a while but I never know when it's going to pop back in. And I don't want it to pop back in. I want it to just be *over*. I'm so tired of this."

"Do you ever wonder why it keeps popping back in?"

"I don't know. I just don't seem to be able to stop it. No, I haven't really wondered *why*. I just want it to stop!"

"Well, stopping it has a lot to do with understanding why. Your body and your mind want you to make sense of it. When you can't make sense of something, it keeps coming back and coming back until you make sense of it. When you make sense of it, the mind says, 'Okay, now you made sense of it so I can put this away now.' But until you do, it just keeps coming to you saying that you didn't make sense of it yet. So that's what you and I are going to do today. We're going to make sense of what happened. It doesn't seem to make any sense, does it?"

"No."

"When you think about it, what is the thought that you have?"

"Well, at first, I really didn't understand. Now I just think this is stupid."

"Here I am. What would you like to ask me about it? Here is Uncle Tom, a grown man—right?"

"Right."

"And he does things that no one else does, right?"

"Right."

"What do you think about that?"

"I don't know why he's picking on *me*."

"Are there other children around for him to pick on?"

"There are now. Now I have a little brother. I don't know if he's doing it to him."

"Maybe he does it to little girls he finds alone. Maybe there are other little girls."

"Yeah, maybe."

"And maybe once he's found one, he doesn't need to do it to the others in the family, you know? There's a word for Uncle Tom. That word is *pedophile*. And that's adult people who do sexual things with children that they aren't supposed to do. Pedophiles come in all different kinds and sizes and shapes and ways that they do it."

"You told me about this at three. And that was really good 'cuz you said they are really sneaky. I couldn't figure out why nobody would help me, and you said 'cuz they're really, really sneaky and they're really, really good at getting little kids alone so there isn't anybody around to help them."

"That's right. And so I said that's why we had to get *you* to be...."

"*Strong!* So I could kick him and stuff. And I get that. But it's the *thoughts* now that are just driving me nuts!"

"So we need to figure out how to stop these thoughts. You need to have a calm, clear mind. So let's go to a moment when you're having this thought, when this experience starts to come up. What's the first thing that comes into your mind?"

"That he's coming toward me. And I think, 'Oh no, not *again*.' And then I start to ... you know I spend a lot of time by myself, right? And I usually have a really good time. I just put myself in all kinds of places. But then, every so often here comes Uncle Tom. And I think, 'Oh no, not *again*.' And then I have to stop what I'm doing and he grabs me and puts me up somewhere so he doesn't have to bend over. And then he does all his stuff. And even if I kick him and get him off—it's more about seeing him coming, walking towards me that's the real 'Oh no, just go *away*.'"

"Well that's where we need to work right now because that's where you need to stop him, Ann."

"Yeah, when he's coming at me I could put up like a shield, like a glass wall or something. And then he wouldn't see it and he'd be coming at me and he'd walk into the wall. And he might even break his nose!"

"I think that's a very good idea," Pamela agreed. "Why don't you try that and let's see what happens. You're playing by yourself and just like what happens every so often, here comes Uncle Tom."

"Right. So there's a little button, and I push the button and the invisible glass wall goes across between him and me. But he doesn't see it, but I know it's there. And he keeps comin' and keeps comin' and it's like the birds that hit the windows in the back of our house all the time. They get knocked out or something. Well, so does he. And then he looks and he looks and then he feels the wall and he's got to walk away because he knows he can't get through. That's really, really good!

"So now I don't even have to worry about him coming at me because I know I just push the button and he's going to hit the wall. And if he does that enough times he won't even come any more because he knows now that I have this glass wall."

"I think that's an excellent plan. Now let's fix it so he can't sneak up on you either."

"Oh yeah. He's never done that, but let's just make sure."

"That inside part of you, show it where the button is. Now close your eyes. And notice when you close your eyes that you can be more aware of what that inside part of you can do. Like it can hear people coming, even when you're playing. It can sense somebody walking up behind you. So you tell that inside part of you any time it senses, hears, sees, *feels* Uncle Tom approaching you, it just presses that button. You show it where that button is."

"It's in my belly button."

"Perfect!"

"Yeah! And even if he gets so close that he grabs one arm, I can still use the other arm to press my belly button."

"That's true. But you know that inside part of you, it can feel and hear him coming from ten feet away. He's not going to get at your arm."

"Oh, good!"

"It's very aware, that inside part of you. It keeps you very safe. It really alarms you and lets you know when there's something you have to pay attention to. How do you think that inside part of you talks to you and lets you know to pay attention?"

"It makes me afraid."

"Right. So let's talk about your body, Ann. And let's talk about your light inside. Because both of them, your body and your light, protect you. Your body has natural instincts, just like a cat or a dog or a lion or a coyote or a wolf. Your body can smell danger coming before you even know it's there. It can hear it. Your inside self can hear much farther than you can—than you know you can. It can smell much better than you think you can. It can hear, see, smell, and feel things.

"So say there's a mountain lion sneaking up on you. Do you know what would happen? Long before you saw or heard the mountain lion the little hairs on the back of your neck and on your arms would go up. That's your body saying, 'Look out, there's a predator, there's a mountain lion sneaking up on us. Pay attention.' And you get a feeling in your stomach, and you get a feeling in your chest and your throat. That would be your body saying, 'Pay attention. I need you to pay attention. There's danger here.' And you feel an adrenalin rush in your body as your legs get really strong to run and your arms get really strong. That body part of you is very, very aware.

"But you also have like a guardian spirit there, too, that talks to you, that warns you, that if you ask a question answers you. I think I talked to the other ages about it being the light inside them. That's what it is. But it's a guardian spirit. It's that light part of you, that part of you that's always with you. It's that part of you that can hold you and comfort you and soothe you. It's that part of you that can talk to you in your mind and tell you if someone is a good person or a bad person."

"Is it like my guardian angel?"

"Right. Churches call it your guardian angel. I call it your light or your Higher Self. But it's the same thing. I think it's more exciting to realize that it's *you, your* power—that *you* have that kind of power, that there is a part of you that is that powerful, that strong, that beautiful, that amazing, and that it's always right there with you. A lot of people can see that part of you. They call it your energy. They'll say, 'Oh! You have marvelous energy!' That's because they're seeing that part of you that is your guardian angel. And it can keep you safe—if you listen to it.

"See, that's the key, Ann. You have to listen to your body, you have to listen to your guardian angel, and trust in them. Trust that your body wants to keep you safe and wants to make you content and strong and happy. And trust that your guardian angel wants what's best for you. Those are really important to know. And nobody can ever take them away from you.

"You have your guardian angel, you have your body, and you have you. And that's your power. You can protect yourself. You can guide yourself. You can feel that love. You're never lost. You're always loved. You always can be strong and powerful if you want to be. Like look what you did with the wall. That was so good! Once you put the wall up, tell me if the thoughts of Uncle Tom go away too."

"Yeah. 'Cuz there's no worry. It can't happen. So I don't have to worry about it. And I think it was worrying about it happening again that made me keep thinking about it."

"Good. Well, it looks like you took care of yourself. I guess that means you can go back to playing happily and not be bothered, right?"

"Yup."

"Good! Then as the five-year-old leaves, let's ask if there's anything that the four-year-old needs to say or wants to know or if this was part of her dilemma too."

My four-year-old comes front and center right away. She's angry with her parents because they aren't there to help her or to protect her. They're always around, even when she doesn't want them around. But when she wants them around, they're not there. They must think it's okay to leave her with Uncle Tom because they wouldn't leave her alone if they knew he was hurting her. But she's still mad.

Pamela explains to the four-year-old that the best way to get answers is to ask questions. The four-year-old finds her parents in the car and asks why they left her alone with Uncle Tom. Pamela asks her how her parents respond.

"Well, they say they left me alone with him 'cuz he's my uncle and he doesn't have any kids and he said he would love to spend a little time with me if they wanted to go out and do something. So they thought, 'Oh, that would be nice.' They're hoping he'll get married and have his own kids, so they figure maybe if they let him spend a little time with me he'll like it and want to get married and have his own kids.

"But he doesn't like kids. I mean, I don't think he likes kids. You don't hurt somebody you like. So I've got to tell them to forget about Uncle Tom liking kids. I tell them, 'When you leave me alone with him, he hurts me; he does bad things to me and then he says not to tell. But I'm telling you anyway because it's the only way I can get you not to leave me alone with him. He gets this funny look on his face and he gets like really strange, and then he starts doing these things to me and . . . just don't leave me alone with him anymore. There's something not right with him.'"

"Are your parents shocked?"

"Yeah. They say, 'What do you mean, he acts strange?' And I say, 'I don't know—just strange. He doesn't act like himself. He acts like somebody else and then he does all this stuff to me and it *hurts*. So just keep him away from me.'

"And they both give me big hugs and say they're really, really sorry. My dad is *really* mad. He's trying not to let me see it, but he's really mad. And my mother, of course, like normal, starts to cry. And they say I was right to tell them and they'll make sure that it never, ever, ever happens again. And they'll be very careful who they leave me alone with. And if anybody ever even gives me a funny feeling I'm s'posed to tell them, no matter what.

"So I feel much better now. And I'm not mad at them 'cuz I saw how upset they were when I told them. They really had no idea. They really thought it was okay."

"What about that mad feeling. Has it gone away?"

"Oh yeah. Now *they're* mad."

"Good! Now let me ask you, Ann, do you feel any kind of shame or guilt or any kind of bad feelings?"

"No, 'cuz they told me I didn't do anything wrong and it wasn't my fault and sometimes grown-ups do that and they're sick. So that's good. No, I don't feel guilty or anything any more."

"Good!" Pamela exclaims. [My four-year-old yawns.] "Looks like it's time to take a nap. That was a lot to get off your chest! That was good. You just feel all good and tingly inside because you've done something very smart and very powerful and very healthy and very good for yourself. I am very proud of you.

"Good. Well done. Then the four-year-old and the five-year-old, with great joy we happily send them into their inner light."

When the regression was over, I started to laugh. "The five-year-old Ann felt so different. She had that hand on her hip saying, 'I'm so over this!' She was such a different personality than the three-year-old, who was still more like a baby and who was mad too but was more like, 'What's happening? Somebody help me.'

"And my four-year-old just needed to hear from mom and dad that they thought it was okay to leave her with Uncle Tom and she hadn't done anything wrong, that they believed her, and they would never leave her alone with Uncle Tom again. Boy, it must be *awful* when parents don't believe a child. I can't even begin to imagine what that must do to the child."

We ended with some NMR to find out if all my molested ages were at peace, which they were. "Well, Pamela," I said, "I think I've said this before, but it's pretty obvious why talk therapy doesn't completely heal abuse. The memories and emotions aren't in the conscious mind. At least the origins aren't. They're at the subconscious level, and all those programs of shame and fear and guilt and powerlessness can only be changed there. Right?"

"Right," Pamela answered.

Some of my little girls did come forward again, but not about sexual abuse. The lesson of the abuse—to reconnect to the power of their own light—had been learned. I had given myself a double whammy in this lifetime, two major opportunities to find my light: adoption and abuse. Yet it's true that the harder the lesson is, the greater the reward. And I'm discovering that connecting to my Higher Self is the greatest reward of all.

CHAPTER 13

THE PRICE OF UNEXPRESSED EMOTIONS

So often people stop short of expressing an emotion out of fear. However, the alternative, repressing an emotion, is always the worse choice, because the emotion festers and eventually surfaces in insidious ways. The key is to understand what the emotion is telling us.

On the drive to Pamela's I suddenly burst into tears. It took me by surprise and I didn't even think it might be a signal. Using NMR at the beginning of the session, we learned that my eight-year-old was crying because she felt unloved.

"You know, Ann," Pamela commented, "the important part of this work is that souls *do* set up experiences, adventures, lessons. So these things happen to children, but souls come along for that ride and to help that child with those experiences. So even though we say divorce and adoption are huge and very difficult for the children, they are also experiences that souls embrace for learning.

"I know I've talked about this many times, but the body is a very important part of your whole life experience. What's important to learn—and many children aren't taught it because *their* parents weren't taught it—is that the body talks to you through its emotions.

"That's why emotions are so very important. They are messages from the body, from the physical, emotional being we refer to as the body. So when we are taught there are certain emotions that are bad or that you shouldn't have or that you don't know what to do with, then we begin to shut down the emotions. We numb our ability to feel. That makes the body very panicky because it's *through* the emotions, it's through those feelings, that the body talks.

"When there's a pain, it's the body saying 'Ouch, pay attention, look around, look at me, what's wrong with me? Something is wrong. Fix it.' We understand that about pain. But sad and mad and scared—these are also messengers, feelings from the body, telling us what's really happening, what's *really* going on, inside.

"Eight-year-olds are very sensitive, very smart, very honest—especially inside. And when they allow themselves to feel what they're feeling and talk about what they're feeling, then it's possible to figure out what's going on with their world, what's happening, and why, so they can make their adjustments and feel happy again, and so they can remember and realize how important they really are."

With Pamela's help, I regress to my eight-year-old, who is feeling sad. Pamela asks her where she feels sad.

"All over." [Sniffling.]

"All over! That's a good description of sad. What does it feel like, all over?"

"Heavy."

"Heavy! Like it's sort of hard to walk around?"

"Yeah."

"Well, I'm sorry to have such a delightful little eight-year-old walking around feeling all heavy and sad. What's making you sad, do you know?"

"My daddy loves my brother, Tommy, more than me."

"Really? Oh, that really *is* a sad feeling! Why do you think so?"

"Because he pays more attention to him."

"Does he always pay more attention to him, or is this something new?"

"No. He always paid lots of attention to me. But now he's paying more attention to him."

"You know, Ann, they're both males, right? Well, males have a thing called male bonding. Females have it too. They call it female bonding. But sometimes daddies really get into that male bonding with their sons. They think there are certain things that males do better than females, and so they want to teach their sons and they want to do things with their sons that they think is male bonding. Daddy is doing male bonding with his son.

"When Tommy was littler, your daddy probably couldn't do that because he couldn't walk as well or talk as well. But now that he's five, daddy is all excited that he can do male bonding with his son and teach him what he needs to do to be a man. And you know what? It may sound silly, but they think they have to do that when the females aren't around. That's why your dad is leaving you out of things.

"And it doesn't sound like he's being smart and sitting down and explaining this to you, is he? You know, Ann, that's a mistake grown-ups make over and over. They don't realize how smart their children are and how much their children would understand if they would just talk to them. It's hard trying to figure it out for yourself, isn't it? You don't know about male bonding if he doesn't talk to you about it.

"And it's possible even your dad doesn't realize what he's doing. He's not seeing how it's affecting his little girl. I bet if he really *knew* how much it was hurting you, he would feel sad, too. Because I don't think he wants you to feel sad. I don't think he knows how sad he's making you feel.

"What happens when your dad and your brother are together? Do you and your mommy do things?"

"Sometimes." [Her voice is weepy.]

"What if you were to go to her and say, 'Mommy, we need to do girl things together.' Then your brother would feel left out, wouldn't he? And you could explain it to him, couldn't you?"

"Uh-huh."

"And when you wanted him to join you, you could say, 'Well this is girl bonding, but these are things boys need to learn too.' And you could say, 'You and daddy are doing things that are boy bonding and I wish I could join you. But that's up to you and daddy.' Then maybe he'd get it in his head sometimes to say to daddy, 'Can Ann come with us too? She likes this.'

"You see what's happening, Ann, is if mom and daddy don't talk to you and your brother about everything that's going on, then you and your brother learn not to talk to each other either. You learn to hold it in. And then when you don't know what's happening and your body feels sad, you don't know what to tell it so it feels better, do you? That's why talking about your emotions, about your feelings, to someone who understands what you're saying is very important. Your sad feeling is telling you what, Ann?"

"That something is wrong."

"Yes. It's saying, 'Something is wrong, I feel left out.' And now what would you say to your body?"

"Well now I'd say, 'Oh body, they're just *bonding*. It's a boy thing."

"Yeah, and they're not smart enough to let me in on it," Pamela added.

"Right. They don't know enough to tell me that they're *bonding*." [She says the word *bonding* with total disgust.]

"'So, I'll just go bond with mom,' right?" Pamela asked. "And maybe you can find special times to do that father/daughter bonding with daddy. What kind of things could you do that maybe even he doesn't think of? What do you and your dad really like to do together?"

"I don't know. But dad and Tommy and I go for rides in the Corvette. And that's the three of us, and that's fun."

"What do you do when dad and Tommy come home from bonding and you're feeling left out? Do you stay in your room?"

"I'm always in my room."

"Maybe sometimes when they come home you could come out and ask them, 'What did you do? Tell me about it,' and show interest in what they did and ask your daddy questions. He likes it when someone is interested in what he does. And communicating is a strong female thing. And then when daddy tells you about something he and Tommy did, if it sounds like fun you could say, 'Oh, that sounds like fun.' And maybe he'd think to say, 'Oh, would you like to do that with us sometime?'

"Because *talking* about it, Ann, will help you a lot. Because then you will be able to understand that your daddy loves you and your daddy loves your brother. And there are many different kinds of love. And your daddy loves your brother like a man loves his son, and your daddy loves *you* like a man loves his daughter. They're both good. And then you and your brother can be closer too. I know sometimes we wish we had our parents all to ourselves. But I'll bet there are some times when you like it that your father and your mother are leaving you alone too, right?"

"Yeah."

"So how is that sad feeling? What's happening with it?"

"Well, I feel like I wouldn't have had to feel sad if they had just told me that they were bonding. When I'm with my mother, we just go *shopping*. That's pretty boring. She calls it girl time. But they get to do fun stuff. I think I was just jealous. I mean, I definitely feel left out but really more jealous. I know daddy still loves me. I thought he just loves Tommy more. But now I get it. He doesn't love Tommy more; he just had to wait for Tommy to grow up to do *bonding*."

"Right. What would have happened if you had said to dad—think about this in your mind—imagine that before we even had this talk that you said to your dad, 'The things you and Tom do together are more fun than what mom and I do together, and when you just want to do them with Tom I feel jealous of that. I feel like you love him more than me.' What if you'd said that? That's what you were thinking. Do you feel safe to tell daddy about your feelings?"

"Now I do."

"And what would he have said to you right then, right there, when you told him that?"

"He probably would have hugged me and said we could do fun things too."

"And wouldn't it have felt good to have him hug you like that and tell you that he *did* love you and he wanted to have fun with you too? Why do you suppose you didn't talk to daddy about that? I'll bet that's another thing called fear. You were afraid if you said it he wouldn't care and you would know he didn't love you. Right? That's when you could talk to yourself and say, 'Oh, I see lots of things my dad does that show me that he loves me.' It's better to find out anyway, isn't it?

"You know, you have an inside part of yourself, Ann, that you can *always* talk to and ask questions of. Like right now you're talking to me inside your mind and asking me questions about that feeling of sadness, of being left out. But if I hadn't been here, there's a part of your very own inside self that is much, much smarter than me. And that part of you loves you very, very much. You know, just like you're always with your body? Well, your inside part is always with *you*. It helps you to understand things. Do you know what part I'm talking about?"

"My light."

"Yes! Do you ever see it?"

"No, I kind of imagine it. It's a *feeling*."

"Okay! What does it feel like?"

"Like somebody's with me."

"Good! So you don't feel alone. Well that light that's with you, you can talk to in your mind. You can even tell that light with you about your feelings. You can say, 'I'm feeling sad, I'm feeling hurt.' Then you can hear in your mind that part talking back to you and helping you understand why you're feeling what you're feeling and helping you feel loved again and special and important and strong and powerful. That feeling is always with you—you always are strong and powerful and special and important.

"And because you feel that way deep inside and that feeling is always with you, then you can look with clear eyes at other people and you can see what's special about them and you can see the mistakes they make without judging them. And then you can know that they don't always know what they're saying and doing and how they're affecting you.

"People really often don't think about what they're doing or what they're saying and how it affects other people. So when someone is mean to you, when somebody says something mean or does something mean or insensitive or says or does something that sounds like they think you aren't as smart as they are or as good as they are, you can say to yourself, 'Hmm, I don't think they really mean that. And even if they do mean it, *I* know that's not true. *I* know who I am, I know how smart I am, I know how special I am, I know everybody isn't exactly alike. So if that person wants me to be exactly like them, maybe that's not right for me at all. Maybe they're not even thinking about who I really am.' And you can think to yourself, '*I'm* going to discover who I am and decide who I want to be and how I want to think about things because I'm smart.'

"And it's true, Ann, you are very, very, *very* smart. And it's also true that you're sensitive, and you can use that sensitivity *for* yourself or *against* yourself. Do you know what I mean by that?

"Like, daddy was going off with your brother, and your sensitive side—you kind of turned it against yourself. You told yourself, 'Oh, he doesn't love me.' But when you use it *for* yourself, then you say, 'Okay, what is daddy trying to do here? Oh, it makes him feel more like a man when he does male bonding. I see. Okay. Poor daddy, he needs more male bonding. All right.'

"Because you really *do* have a sensitivity, Ann. You really *do* have a wonderful ability to be able to talk to people in a way that uses their terms and their words. And that helps them to understand what you're talking about. That's a wonderful talent that you have. And it's going to serve you really, really well for all the years of your life.

"But you have to remember, as good as you are at talking to other people, you have to be that good—even better—at talking to yourself. Because your self needs you. Your body needs you to help it understand and to help it feel good and to help it feel strong and to help it feel powerful, and to help it feel loved. When you pay attention to what your body is feeling, and when you talk to it about what it's feeling in a way that makes it feel good, then it feels loved. It feels it's not all alone, it feels important.

"Just think about it, Ann. Your body will have you its whole life. You won't leave it behind. You won't betray it. You won't reject it. You won't try to make it feel bad. You'll be here to take care of it, to love it, and show it respect. And that body that's listening to you is thinking right now, 'Oh, that feels good.'

"And you, eight-year-old, you are such an important part of this lifetime. Even the grown-up you wouldn't be where she is without you. You're an important part of that sensitivity. You know the grown-up Ann, when she's grown up, there's an actor and an actress who go through a very messy divorce, and the actress says about him, 'You know what's wrong him? He's missing the sensitivity chip.'

"Well, no one can say that about the grown-up Ann. You know why? Because you're her sensitivity chip! You're the sensitivity chip—or child or mind or personality or whatever you want to call it, eight-year-old. You're the part that helps so much with her purpose of making people understand themselves—and through that, understanding others, and through that, understanding the world. And to understand themselves people have to understand about their minds and their spirits and their bodies. And that takes sensitivity. That takes what you have taught your soul.

"Speaking of your soul, eight-year-old, you know that part that I said looks like a light and you said you feel it? It wants you with it now. It wants you to be with it every moment, so every moment you are loved. So if you would just close your eyes and think about being loved and then being held by that part, you can feel that light all around you and inside of you filling you up completely, and it's just the most wonderful, euphoric, happy, joyful feeling. Just move right into that feeling."

After the regression I had to laugh. "Boy, she didn't think much of male bonding, did she? Every time she used the word it was with such disgust! That was pretty cute! And I loved how you explained the mistake parents make of not talking to their children about things. And she didn't tell her daddy she was feeling left out because she was afraid he wouldn't care. What did you call that? Using your sensitivity against yourself instead of for yourself. That was really good.

This regression made me think of all the times I'd heard parents say, "Oh, it doesn't matter. He, or she, is too young to understand what's going on." But a child is never too young. As I discovered in an earlier session, even a fetus needs to know what is really going on. It is when children understand what is happening that they can feel free to express what they really feel.

CHAPTER 14

DON'T TRADE ME IN

Because children can easily misunderstand what is happening around them, they are susceptible to taking on all kinds of emotional programs. In this regression, two inner ages who have been traumatized by a misunderstood thought come forward. My infant thinks mommy doesn't love her, and my three-year-old thinks she's going to be traded in for a new baby. Both ages feel unloved. Helping them to understand the true situation and change their response allows me to alter the thought and the resulting emotional program.

"Oh, Pamela," I said before I even hit The Chair, "now something is happening in my shoulder. I feel like someone or something is grabbing at me right here, right here in the trapezius. It's different from the old stabbing pain. This is something new. I guess my subconscious is saying, 'Here's another one for you.' I never knew I had so much stuff! Let's find out what it is."

With NMR we learned the issue was fear when I was three and my parents adopted my brother. On a hunch, I asked if my three-year-old was afraid they were going to trade her in. The answer was yes.

"Whoa, I don't know where that question came from!"

"Possibly your Higher Self, Ann?"

"Oh. Thank you, Higher Self."

"So, you are three, there's a new baby coming, and you're afraid they're going to trade you in," Pamela summarized. "I think we need to talk to that three-year-old." Then she said, "I just received a message from *my* Higher Self to talk to the infant as well. So we'll do that first."

"Okay. Take a deep breath . . . and as you relax deeper and deeper and deeper into that feeling, you allow yourself to let go and just drift into that lightness of being, lighter and lighter and lighter. That's perfect. That means you can go back there to . . . let's see, there's a nursery with an infant to talk to and there's a three-year-old to talk to.

"Now, adult Ann, imagine you're holding the infant you."

"I'm holding this infant," I said in my adult voice. "And somehow I know how to hold her and not be afraid of her or be afraid I'm going to hold her wrong or afraid I'm going to drop her. It feels natural, not foreign. And she's so happy to have someone hold her who makes her feel safe. She's looking up at me, and she feels calm and safe, like she belongs in my arms, like she just belongs. She doesn't feel like she's some kind of foreign object."

"Good. Let me talk to that infant a minute as you're holding her there in your arms. 'Little infant girl Ann, let me talk to you a moment. Feels good there in those arms holding you, doesn't it?'"

"Umm,'" she said, all weepy and sniffling.

"Feels safe, huh? She says you feel like you belong. Is that right?"

"Umm."

"Yes, you do. You very much belong. You know, that's the older you, the adult you, that's holding you. When your mommy who adopted you holds you, how does she hold you?"

"Like a board. Like she's afraid of me."

"You know, she isn't afraid of *you*; she is afraid she might drop you or hurt you. She's never held a little baby in her arms before, and she doesn't quite know how to do it, so it makes her very, very nervous. I know you pick up on that nervous feeling and her nervous thoughts. How might you help your mommy not feel so nervous? Let's go to a moment when mommy, in your mind, is holding you. And oh, she's nervous and scared. Now that I've told you it's not you she's scared of, see if you can find a way to help mommy relax. Can you talk to her in your mind? You know she has a lot of nervous thoughts and feelings, but can you get through to her?"

"I can tell her she's doing great and if she can relax it would be even better. I mean, I don't cry or anything. *I'm* not making her think she should be nervous."

"Well let's see what would help her to relax. Can you make any happy sounds, infant, some cooing sounds or giggling sounds? Let's see if you can do that, if you can relax in mommy's arms and make some cooing, giggling sounds. And while you're doing it, you know, baby, there's a light inside you. Do you think you can shine it on mommy? You need to find that light and grow it really big, and shine it on mommy so she sees you smiling in her mind's eye. She hears you cooing and giggling. She feels your little body relax. And what happens when you do this?"

"I understand I have the power here."

"Yes, you do!"

"I've got to make *her* relax instead of her making *me* relax."

"That's right! That's brilliant! You have the power there, baby girl. You just concentrate on helping her to relax. You tell her in your mind, 'That's okay, mommy. I will help you.

We'll do this together. You chose me, but I chose you, too. We belong together. We're going to get through this just fine because we belong here together.' Tell her that. Reassure her. Say, 'Mommy, I'll let you know if I'm not comfortable. I'll cry or I'll whimper and that will let you know.'

"Now, baby girl, I need to tell you something. This woman who is your mother and this father who brought you home are going to keep you. The adoption papers are done. They're not going to take you back. They need you to let them know when you're comfortable or not comfortable. When they put you in your crib, if you're hot or sticky or wet or hungry or uncomfortable, you need to whimper or cry to let them know.

"And pretty soon they're going to start to figure out: Oh, *that* cry means she's wet. Oh, *that* cry means a pin is poking her. Oh, *that* cry means she's not really tired. Oh, *that* cry means she's overtired. You see? By you altering just slightly the way you cry, they're going to start picking up the message in your mind of what's wrong and what they need to do to fix it.

"But they need to hear from you. They need you to use your voice and your body to communicate to them what you need from them. They wanted you very, very much. And now they're learning how to feel safe and comfortable with you and how to help you feel safe and comfortable. But *you've* got to let *them* know. You need to speak up the way a baby infant can. So you have happy sounds and not-happy sounds. And you help train them to know what sound means what. Can you do that?"

"Yeah, as long as I know they're not going to take me back."

"Well, I want you to close your eyes and do something very special, which I think you have the ability to do. Close your eyes and look two years ahead in time. You see that time line right there. Look along it two years ahead in time and tell me, do you see yourself with them?"

"Uh-huh."

"Okay. Look four years ahead in time. Just keep moving up that line. Are you still with them?"

"Uh-huh."

And now you're eight. Are you still with them?"

"Uh-huh."

"And now you're fifteen. Are you still there?"

"Uh-huh."

"And eighteen—see? They're not taking you back. It's set. They wanted you, they got you, and they're going to keep you. You chose them. They chose you. Nothing, no one, can separate you. It's done! You are theirs. They are yours. You are their family. They are your family. You belong here. They will take care of you. To them, in their minds—look in and see if I'm correct—you are their baby, their daughter. They will let *no one* take you away from them.

"And that means you can cry at the top of your lungs and they're not going to think, 'Oh, we have to take her back.' They're going to think, 'Oh my goodness, what is she so upset about? Let's find out so we can fix it.' You need to let them know that your body feels good or not good. And it's the same with your feelings. You're important. You matter. Does all that ring true with you, little one?"

"Uh-huh."

"Good. You can *feel* that? Now can you imagine being cranky because you're too hot and so you let them know that?"

"Yeah."

"And they come in and oh, their baby infant is all fussy and crying and it's the middle of the night, and what do they do?"

"They fix it. And I know I can do that and they won't send me away."

"Good! Tell me, infant, little one, check your feelings inside, is there any part of you that is still feeling unsafe? Uncomfortable? No? Are you feeling pretty good?"

"Yeah."

"Great. Now imagine in your mind that you're in a nursery and this nursery is full of light. It's a nursery of light. Does that feel comfortable for you?"

"Yes."

"As the infant girl, move into that light and feel all that brightness and happiness and joy, and tell me if that's a comfortable place for you to be."

"Yeah. I see now that I'm here to help them just like they're here to help me."

"Good. Very good. So we leave the infant there with her light self and now we're looking for the three-year-old. Is that you, three-year-old?"

A three-year-old voice responded, "It's okay now that they're getting another baby because I know I'm safe. I can even help them with the new baby. I mean, I've *already* helped them with the new baby, because now mommy isn't going to be so afraid when she holds the new baby so there won't be that problem. And I know they're not going to trade me in for the new baby 'cuz I'm here for good. And I'll help the new baby know that he or she is here for good. I don't want the new baby to have to feel like I felt 'cuz that sucks!"

"That's right! You can even talk to that new baby—and by the way, it's going to be a brother. You can talk to that brother in his mind just like you talked to mommy and daddy in their minds. You talk to that baby brother and you just give him the whole scoop—what kind of sounds to make that mom and dad already understand. And maybe he can experiment with some of his own. And you just tell him, 'You know, they're not sending you back. I'm their daughter, you're their son.

These people *keep* their children. These people never give their children away.'

"And you just tell him, 'You can express what you're feeling—you can be angry, you can be sad, you can cry, you can be happy—you can just be yourself because you will always be here. We'll be brother and sister for always.' That's a *very* good, important role for you, three-year-old. You really are the helper. You really are helping mom and dad and brother and yourself. Now you know how important you are, don't you? You're kind of a key to all this."

"Yeah. And I can tell him he doesn't have to be perfect for them to keep him."

"And you know that because. . . ."

"Because I found out I don't have to be perfect anymore."

"That's right. You don't have to be perfect anymore. Can you imagine anybody being perfect? What is perfect? Ugh! That's an impossible thing, isn't it?"

"Well, it's really kind of pretending to be perfect. It *is* pretending to be perfect."

"Yes, it is pretending to be perfect. And that's no fun, to keep pretending that, is it?"

"No, it's not."

"So now you know that you can be exactly who and what you are, which is wonderful, which is great! Let's see, you're three now. Does mommy feel comfortable with you now?"

"Uh-huh."

"And is she relaxed enough that you can feel mommy's love now?"

"*Now,* yes, 'cuz I know she's not taking me back."

"Can you feel daddy's love, too?"

"Oh yeah!"

"Oh good. Do you think you can start to remind adult Ann of happy memories from when you're three years old? Like the day they bring your brother home—do you remember that day?"

"No."

"I bet you could, three-year-old. Just close your eyes and go to the day when there's some kind of excitement in the air. Something *different* is happening in your family. It's the day they bring home the new baby. That day begins to gather in your mind. What impressions are gathering there?"

"I'm home with somebody who is taking care of me 'cuz they went on a trip to get a new baby. I think I'm excited."

"Okay, so you're excited. Do you hear them first or see them first?"

"I'm still in the house when they come in with the baby."

"What happens when they come in with the baby?"

"They let me see it."

"What are you thinking? Can you talk to the baby in your mind right away?"

"I'm thinking I'm going to have to share my mommy and daddy with this . . . thing."

"And now can you look at your baby brother differently?"

"Oh yeah. Now I look at him like a doll I can take care of." [She laughs.]

"Okay. Very good, three-year-old. Are you feeling comfortable? Are you feeling content?"

"Oh yeah. I'm feeling *much* better."

At this point we returned to the adult me to heal my shoulder. I focused on the sensation of a bunch of little fingers jabbing right there on my trapezius. It's funny that those children chose my trapezius, my trap, because it was like a trap—they were trapped until I let them out. Pamela asked me to focus on the trapped energy leaving and to think, "I don't have to hold on to the past anymore." After coming back to conscious awareness, I commented, "My shoulder is so much better, I can't believe it! And my three-year-old—that was so emotional. I got all teary when she found out she didn't have to be perfect because they weren't going to take her back.

"What is really interesting is that I could tell myself that from now 'til doomsday at the conscious level and it really wouldn't do any good. I guess that's why people go to shrinks for years and years and for the most part never do clean up their stuff. And I cleaned that one up in an hour. Wild!"

"Yes," Pamela responded. "But it can take more than one regression. It all depends on how resistant the program is. Sometimes it can take two or three or even four sessions. Once in a while it can take even more than that. Everyone is different, and every issue is different."

After this regression I kept feeling sad for those two inner ages who experienced themselves as unloved and carried all that fear of not being perfect, and of being traded in. But then I would remember why those ages went through those experiences—so I could learn. It was all okay. It all happened for a reason.

Chapter 15

ANGELS AND DREAMS

Dream experts tell us that everyone dreams. However, not everyone remembers their dreams. Why is that? And what about psychic experiences? Supposedly we're all capable of them, so why do some people have them and others don't? In today's regression I find answers to both questions.

"I think I've mentioned before that I don't dream," I said to Pamela. "But somewhere along the way I learned we dream every night, that we leave our bodies at night to lower its vibration so it can repair and restore what needs to be done, and that dreams are an account of where we go and what we do on those adventures. If this is true, why don't I remember my dreams? I mean, I remember them once in a while, like maybe two or three times a year.

"Also, I don't have any psychic experiences," I went on. "I want to see auras and hear spirit communication and stuff like that. So I want to find out what's blocking that, too."

NMR revealed that my psychic experiences were blocked because I was suppressing childhood memories of communicating with spirit. The nuns who taught kindergarten had caught my five-year-old talking to her spirit friends and told her it was wrong, so she became afraid of communicating with spirit. We needed to talk to my five-year-old. I also learned that I did dream frequently, I just didn't recall my dreams because of something that happened in seventh grade. So we needed to visit my seventh-grader, too.

First we talked to my five-year-old. We found her in kindergarten, and the nuns were there. "The nuns talk to you about a lot of things—is that true?" Pamela asked.

"Yeah," a five-year-old voice responded, "they mostly make up things for us to do and ways for us to play together. This is really the first time I've been around other kids to play. I'm not quite sure about it. Mom just brought me here one day and dropped me off and left. I didn't like it very much, but then I got used to it. My friends are here with me, all the friends that I talk to that nobody else can see. They're still the ones I like the best."

"Do they come to school with you?"

"Oh yeah. I wouldn't come without them."

"What do they do when you're studying? Do they study too?"

"They're just here. We don't study, really. We draw and stuff like that. And they're right here with me."

"Do you talk to them out loud sometimes?"

"Yeah."

"And so what happens when you talk to them out loud and no one else can see them? Does anyone ever say anything?"

"Well, I don't talk to them very loud, see, and most of the kids don't pay any attention. They either think I'm talking to somebody else or they don't really care. It's the grown-ups that care. They say that talking to my friends is bad. They say there's nobody there and that you can't talk to someone who isn't there.

"I say yes, there's somebody there. It's my friends. And they say, but there's nobody there—look, look. And they go through all this stuff to show me there's nobody there, and they say it's wrong. And I say, well, what if it's my guardian angels that I'm talking to?

"And they say, 'You can't talk to your guardian angels. Your guardian angels are there to protect you, but you don't *talk* to your guardian angels.'

"And I say, 'Well, I talk to *my* guardian angels. And my guardian angels talk to *me*.' And this big tall nun in this funny-looking dress says, 'No, no, that can't be, and you'd better stop that or people are going to think you're crazy and will make fun of you. And you'll get punished.'

"So I stop because I don't want to get in trouble. I still talk to them at home because then I'm all by myself and nobody knows. But now I'm a little nervous about it. I don't really believe I'm doing something wrong, but I can't do it at school, so even when I talk to my friends at home, it isn't as much fun."

"Do your spirit friends stop going to school with you when you stop talking to them at school?"

"That's a good question. I think I leave them at home because what's the point, you know? I figure maybe I'm getting big now and I've got to learn to do things on my own. At school we have a little post office and we play games, and I think maybe I can learn to play with some kids that are, like, *there*. Because next year I've gotta start with books and really learning things, and that's gonna be with other kids. So maybe this is like some kind of entranceway into that world. Maybe my other friends should be my at-home friends."

"Do any of them ever say anything about the big nun in the funny-looking dress saying that they weren't really there and that it's bad to see them?"

"I don't know if they say anything, but they just kind of let me know—I'm not quite sure how—I just kind of know I wasn't like really, really bad or anything like that. I just can't do it at school because they don't like it. I think the nuns are wrong, but they don't like it so I just don't do it in front of them. It's like everything else. If they don't like it, I still do it. I just don't do it in front of them. I don't like that, but hey, you gotta do what you gotta do."

"Very good. Now close your eyes and leave that kindergarten. Go to a place where your friends are gone. Where are you now?"

"I'm in seventh grade. [This voice is more mature.] "I feel like I'm out in the world now and I've got things to do after school. I have other friends now, so my imaginary friends aren't around me any more. I don't really miss them. I feel like their time is over."

"And when you go to sleep at night, what's happening with your dreams?"

"I dream about boys. I dream about the boys I want to like me."

"And what happens when you dream about them?"

"They like me!"

"In your dreams?"

"Yeah."

"Does that happen in real life?"

"No. Different ones like me but not the ones I dream about."

"Do you know that dreams are symbolic?"

"No."

"They are."

"But these guys are real, they're real people," I insist.

"Well, they're *representing* your wanting to be loved. The boys that you like and want to have like you in your dreams represent your desire to be loved."

"Yeah, I can see that."

"When we're children, our parents don't teach us about our dream world and how to know the language of the dream world because *they* don't know, because humans have pretty much forgotten it. Do you know why? When churches came along, in an effort to control, they didn't want people getting messages from inside themselves."

"They took all that away from us."

"Exactly. They did. And so humans forgot it for a long time. But here we are remembering it again. And here you are at the age of twelve learning that your dreams are an important way to talk to you about what's going on inside *you*, because what's going on inside *you* is what affects your outer world. It makes things happen when they happen. It's important that you feel, inside yourself, that you are worthy of love, that your feelings matter, that you are a good person, and that life has good things in store for you. Do you know why your birth mother gave you up for adoption?"

"Because she was married to someone else."

"That's right. She hadn't really met you yet. She wasn't really paying attention to her inner self. So even though you were talking to her in your mind while you were inside her, she wasn't listening, really. She knew she had to give you up, so she was really closing that off. She didn't give you up because she didn't like you, or couldn't love you. She couldn't keep you.

"Then your mother and father adopted you. They wanted to have a little girl, and they picked you out of all the other babies. However, some people find it much easier to show love than other people. And I think your mom and dad find it harder to show love."

"The physical part, yes, definitely."

"So you felt that separation, that rejection. Babies love to be held and touched and hugged. And that doesn't go away when we're twelve. We act like it does, but it doesn't. We still like to be held and hugged and to sit close."

"And this is the age," I said, "where you *can* be. You can make out and sit on a couch with someone's arm around you. So that's probably why I'm dreaming about these boys."

"Right. Your inside self knows what's missing. And it's actually figured out a clever way to say 'Okay, let's give it to you in your dreams, even while we're giving you a message, so you feel held close. Because maybe you haven't been taught about boundaries yet, so this way you don't get into trouble in school, or with the boys, either. That's the glory of dreams.

"And that's why I'm talking to you. The choice you make now about dreams affects you the rest of your life. Earlier, you made a decision—what's the use of dreaming when dreams don't come true?—because you didn't know what dreams are really about. But now you do know what dreams are about. So I'm asking what you think about dreaming for the rest of your life: Do you want to do it, or do you not want to do it?"

"Oh, I do!"

"Good, because that changes everything. And now that the grown-up you knows about dream language, you'll know what to do with dreams, too. Bring your dreams to your Higher Self, because the Higher Self can interpret them.

"Thank you, twelve-year-old. Talking to you was really important, and now, as you return into your joy, into your light, that's good.

"So now, adult Ann, let's go to that blackboard in your mind. Right there on the board erase: 'I don't want to remember my dreams.' Erase: 'It is bad to talk to spirit, it is a sin to communicate with or be in the world of spirit.' Erase: 'I will be punished for talking to spirits and listening to spirits.' Erase: 'It's frustrating to dream. I don't want to do it.'

"You replace the old thinking with new thoughts. You write on that blackboard: 'My dreams are important to me. I desire to know my dreams, to remember them. I use my dreams for counsel, for guidance. I use my dreams to review events and understand them. It is *good* to dream. It is *good* to communicate responsibly with spirit. I am in connection with my guardian angel. I *do* hear my guardian spirit, my Higher Self. My Higher Self, my guardian spirit, *does* talk to me. The nuns were wrong and I was right. My Higher Self, which is my intuitive, spiritual self, my guardian angel, guides me, and I hear and pay attention to its voice.'"

After hypnosis, Pamela talked a little more about dreams. "People don't pay attention to their dreams, yet that's where the Higher Self is talking to us big-time. Spirit communicates through the mind. It uses the language of the mind, which is symbolic imagery. Ninety-nine percent of the images we see in our dreams represent something about the dreamer, an aspect of the dreamer, or an aspect of the dreamer's relationship with another person in the dream.

"These images and their symbolic meaning are different for each of us. As you begin to recall your dreams, their meaning will become apparent to you. Keep a pad or a recorder by your bed, and as soon as you wake up, just record anything— I feel groggy, I feel disgruntled, I'm certain I had a dream, I wish I knew what my dream was—just *anything* to get in the habit of recording it. This starts attuning your subconscious to the fact that you want the dreams, that you want to know what you dreamt."

After this session, I started recalling more of my dreams. I also learned to interpret my dream images. Now when I can't figure out the symbolism of a dream, I ask my Higher Self. Many of my dreams are messages of encouragement. Others are messages of guidance. Sometimes a catastrophic experience in a dream is really about my ability to overcome it. After this session I also started to focus on seeing and hearing things in the non-physical world. Little by little, I'm developing that skill.

Chapter 16

HIDDEN MARRIAGE PROGRAMS

When a person's marriage is unhappy or ends in divorce, the assumption is that he or she must have married the wrong person. But perhaps the problem lies in a subconscious belief that happiness is impossible in any marriage. In this session I learn that my beliefs about marriage originated in an incident at age eight—which is also the source of the thought that triggered my poor eyesight program.

On the day of this session with Pamela, my eyesight was unusually blurry. I'd been writing a film treatment about a marriage. The more I wrote, the blurrier my eyes got.

We learned with NMR that my blurry eyesight was a signal from my eight-year-old that she wanted to talk. She was distressed because her parents were arguing about her father's Corvette.

"Ah! Dad had this little 1953 Corvette," I explained. "He loved that car. He was like a big kid with a new toy. He had this wooden bench made to fit over the console so all four of us could ride in it. When it was just dad and my brother and me, Tom would sit on the bench and I'd sit in the passenger seat. But on Sundays, when mom came with us, I had to sit on that horrible little bench with my head sticking up over the windshield, and Tom had to sit in Mom's lap. Neither one of us liked that arrangement at all. So on Sundays, we'd say with a great degree of un-enthusiasm, 'Oh, mom, are *you* coming?' which of course she didn't like one bit. So finally she said, 'Cecil, it's me or that car!' I always thought it was a joke.

"So one day he came home with a four-passenger convertible so we would all fit. It was a cool car, but it wasn't his beloved Corvette. But I don't remember that as a fight. I only remember her saying, 'Cecil, it's me or that car.' She was much more conservative than he was. I think she held him back."

More NMR revealed that I was still carrying anger and fear from that event. I was also blocking some of what was said.

"But what's the problem, then, here today, Ann? Is it upsetting your thoughts about marriage? Is it making you fearful about relationships? Does it interfere with your trusting of relationships?"

We did more NMR, which disclosed that today's blurry eyesight resulted from my not wanting to see something. I also learned that I was afraid a marriage where both people are free to be themselves was impossible and this made me angry.

"So what's the part you're afraid can't happen? Where's the fear?" Pamela asked.

"Well, I always *thought* they were so happy. I never heard them fight. So I thought you never argued in marriage, that you agreed on everything. And then I find out, at least at the subconscious level, that isn't true. But I can't believe I really thought they'd get divorced over that car. I just remember mom saying, 'It's me or that car.' I always saw that as a joke. But I guess there are things I don't remember about that conversation."

NMR confirmed that in fact I hadn't seen it as a joke. I had believed her. I thought she was going to leave my father. I knew my dad was angry about her ultimatum, and his anger frightened me. I felt bad for my father and was angry at my mother. This anger and fear was affecting my feelings about marriage. Moreover, after that incident I started to believe my parents didn't love each other and wanted to be free of each other—and *I didn't want to see that.*

"This is heavy duty for an eight-year-old to think about," Pamela explained. "It would be hard for her to hear, 'There's a possibility they've grown apart. There's a possibility they're not compatible. There's a possibility they've entangled themselves so much in their own personal stuff that they've deadened what they felt between them.' This is the reality of human nature—that we aren't static, that we grow and change.

"We might start talking to the eight-year-old about what keeps marriages together and what causes marriages to die. And we might say to her, 'Can you imagine what might be an important key between any two people in keeping a marriage honest to what it is and to keeping a marriage flourishing, or to ending the marriage if both parties would be happier?' The strongest key to keeping them together—something your parents lacked, at least to a degree, Ann—is *communication.* Not only communication with each other but communication with oneself.

"You're getting your first big dose of how important it is to look inward, to recognize very basic things that an amazing amount of people don't know, like: 'Who am I? What do *I* want? What is meaningful and important to me, and how am I getting in the way of that?' Not 'How are others getting in the way?' but 'How am *I* getting in the way?' 'Am I not being honest with myself? Am I making choices based on what I think other people think should be my choices?'

"Your mom and dad have done a *lot* of that. How old were they when they got married?"

"Thirty. They were forty when they adopted me."

"So they were forty-eight now. That's interesting, that they had a longer time to get to know themselves. And at that age there's already a panic, starting with, 'I haven't done what I wanted to do. Is life just going to continue to be the same, the same, the same?' All that is happening. And so one of the things we want to say to the eight-year-old is, 'If you're going to look within yourself, you have to be willing to face what's there.' And in your parents' day and age there weren't a whole lot of options for them. It was the 1950s and they were *very* tied by what was expected by society. So it was very hard to step out of the mold. What's your mom going to do at age forty-five if she hasn't worked?"

"Oh no. She ran four corporations. Dad knew he was going to die young because he had rheumatic fever as a child, so he set her up to have income after he died. And she loved business. She was a very astute businesswoman. But he knew he was going to die around his mid-fifties, which he did, although it was from cancer.

"He used to come home from work and he'd be dog-tired, and he'd sit in this recliner and he was always wiggling his big toe. I remember she was always darning his socks in the toe. He was always wiggling that big toe. Always. I guess it was nerves. So there was a lot of nervous energy there. It was probably total frustration. Let me ask about my father wiggling his toe."

NMR revealed dad did wiggle his toe as a release of nervous energy. The cancer that killed him was from frustration and anger.

"So," Pamela explained, 'here is an opening to say to the eight-year-old that this is another reality that she needs to look at. Let's say she was here being counseled and needs to be opened up to: You're beginning to recognize that you are an individual, your mother is an individual, your father is an individual. And there are bonds created with individuals but you can't solve your parents' problems. You can't make your mother happy. You can't make your father happy. And what happens between them is of course going to affect you, but you can't let it throw you.

"You're now going to have to look at your parents also as teachers. And they are *teaching* you, showing you choices. You can look at your parents and begin to see them for the fallible human beings they are who have made choices, and decide for yourself if the choices they have made are choices that feel good to you. Your mother is showing you choices, your father is showing you choices, and one of the things they are showing you is the consequences of lack of communication and the consequences of suppressing emotions and the consequences of having the fear of showing a partner who you are and discussing with a partner what you want.

"So what would you say to the eight-year-old to help her dissipate her anger at mother?" Pamela asked. "She's angry at mother for not letting father be who he is and play and have fun."

I responded: "I'd say, 'Your mother was raised in a very conservative household and there was a lot of fear there. She never saw anybody let go and be themselves and have the freedom to express who they really were. That just wasn't something *known* to her. That scared her. Then she marries this adventurous type. At first it's very appealing to her and she thinks she's going to be able to go with the flow, but she just can't do it. So she gets miserable and he gets miserable. They're both unhappy. But she really did think she'd be able to go with it at first.'"

"So," Pamela said, "by telling the eight-year-old this, you help her see how easily her parents slipped into those roles and probably were angry at themselves, frustrated and angry at themselves."

"But not really knowing they were angry with themselves, thinking that they were angry with the other," I added.

"So we're telling the eight-year-old about projection," Pamela explained, "that when you can't really face choices, failures, unhappiness that *you've* made, you project it onto others—this frustration and this anger—and you get angry at *them* in the very area that you're still trying to resolve. So now let's test some programs about marriage with the subconscious."

NMR revealed that I considered living with someone a marriage, and that I thought you're not allowed to be who you want to be in marriage and that marriage is a dependent relationship.

"That's pretty much the nuts and bolts, Ann: not being allowed to express yourself and being dependent. What we're looking at is the framework you've built as your matrix of marriage so we can dismantle it."

We tested further for programs and found two. One was that marriage made both men and women unhappy. The other was that whereas I liked being a female and respected females, I did not admire or respect female energy. I saw female energy as domineering, controlling, and judgmental. I did not see male energy this way.

"You sided with your dad a lot. I think you kind of dissed yourself thinking, 'I'm not going to be at all like my mother,' which may have dissed some female stuff. Things don't have to make sense at the subconscious level. And here you have two opposing ideas. You respect females but you don't admire them. Let's do a little bit of reprocessing."

Pamela started the now-familiar induction procedure. "Then as you close your eyes, you begin that process that works for you: counting down, the numbers five and down to four, that's it, focusing in on your body at three. Because we are working with the subconscious programs, you do want to go at two, into those levels within. So you're thinking of the body at one, as you go to the screen of your mind.

"That blackboard is how you inform your subconscious. And as we look at the blackboard now, there's something about female energy there. It says female energy is domineering, female energy is controlling, female energy is judgmental. And I'll bet if you look at it closely it says *all* female energy, because no one bothered to inform the subconscious otherwise.

"Erase the 'all' and put 'some' in front of it. Because that is true. In fact, erase 'energy' because *some* females are domineering—they use their female energy in a domineering, controlling, judgmental way. All right. But now you pick up that chalk and you write: 'My mother was a female. My mother had female energy. I am a female. I have female energy.' And then write in big, bold letters: 'All female energies are not the same. Female energy is different in different females. I am not my mother. I use my female energy differently than my mother did. Many, many, *many* females use their energy differently than my mother did.'

"And that goes right to that programmer to direct those changes in the emotional programming, the fundamental programming. And you also write on that board: 'Female energy is strong. Females can communicate. I choose to be that kind of female.'"

"Now erase: 'Don't show your emotions.' Erase: 'It's better not to show your emotions so everyone will think everything is all right.' Then write: 'My emotions signal to me what I need to know about what I am feeling and thinking. When my emotions signal me, I know what to do about it. I address what's important for me to address so I keep myself balanced, powerful, and on my path of purpose, my path of destiny.'

"Good. And now, Ann, you go to the other side of the board and there it is written: 'Marriage is a prison.' 'Marriage doesn't allow one to be oneself.' 'Marriage is a dependent relationship.' 'Marriage makes men and women unhappy.'

"This is true of some marriages. But it is not true of marriage itself, which can be many things. So erase: 'Marriage is a prison.' We don't want this to be true for you. Erase the others as well. They do not need to be true for you. And by erasing them, you are letting your subconscious know that you have made different opinions, different thoughts about marriage.

"So you write on that board: 'Marriage is a reflection of the people that are in it. Marriage is a good opportunity to communicate clearly, honestly, with consideration and respect for the opinions and the thoughts and the feelings of both partners. Communication is important for me. Communication is important in a marriage.'

"You might also write: 'Marriage can free a person to be who that person is. Marriage *can* allow one to be oneself. Marriage can be a union between two independent people who care for one another and create a bond together. Marriage *can* help men and women to be happier with themselves and with their lives. Marriage is many things to many people.'

"I suggest at some point, Ann, that you might lean back, put yourself into that hypnotic state, and begin stating aloud or silently the positive beliefs that you want to make certain your subconscious has accepted as your belief system about marriage and other things that matter to you. Make certain you've imprinted that for yourself and that your subconscious has received it and that your subconscious programming supports what you have come to think, believe, and know at your conscious level of understanding and awareness.

"Now, taking another deep breath, we thank the eight-year-old for her contribution, for communicating. When you were writing about marriage, she began communicating. She began saying, 'Hey, I have some thoughts, I have some feelings about this that have been bugging me for a long time. Can I talk to you about them?' And you did talk about them together. Congratulations to both of you.

"As you reflect on and recognize the choices that have been made, you make a conscious decision to make the conscious choices that matter to you, that embrace your higher good, that embrace your greater satisfaction. You are indeed in the process of empowering yourself, of removing those limitations that you have placed on yourself so that you can, in this realm, find, enjoy, and master this realm and become that light of joy, joy, joy that is your essence.

"Now breathing in that physical energy, and as you bring in that physical energy, reflect to yourself before we are done that you are pushing out *all* the energies of your mother and of your father and *all* the energies of all entities that your Higher Self and you know do not belong with you—the negative energies, the belief systems that are not what you have chosen. You are embracing that energy of Ann. You are embracing that energy of *your* light, that energy of *your* spirit. You are surrounding yourself and making yourself very, very comfortable with, comfortable in, balanced in the energies of your spiritual soul, of your being. And this includes your emotions. This includes your physical energies, for you are embodied in physical form. How wonderful to know that indeed we have the power to motivate ourselves, to heal ourselves, to inspire ourselves, to find the knowledge we are seeking within self."

What a shock this regression was! I had always thought my parents were so happy. They never argued. They were always holding hands in their photos. Not wanting to see their unhappiness was what triggered the old program about eyesight from the first century. My parents were counterexamples—through their unhappiness they taught me good lessons: find the strength in who you truly are so you feel free to express it, and don't blame others if you haven't. I'll have to keep you posted on whether or not this session helped me with marriage. But I can tell you it has helped me with relationships in general.

CHAPTER 17

THE PURPOSE OF AN EVIL LIFE

If everything has a spiritual reason, then what about negatives—do they have a spiritual purpose too? Specifically, what is the reason for evil? Why does a soul sometimes choose to live an evil life?

"I just had a *terrible* weekend," I told Pamela as I settled into The Chair. "Friday I got a huge bill that totally blew my budget. I thought I would have to use therapy money to pay it, so I called you and cancelled my appointment for today. And that was the beginning of the downhill slide.

"No matter what I did, I just felt awful. So I decided to use the Higher Self induction tape you made for me. I thought, 'I'm going to have a little chat with my Higher Self.' Well! Every time I started the induction, I would just burst into tears. At first I thought maybe it was all the crying I didn't do as a kid because I thought I had to be so stoic. But then after several times I was thinking: I don't *feel* the cool air, I don't *feel* the lightness. I'm just a big *fraud*. And I'd burst into tears!

"Then Monday morning I woke up and decided it doesn't matter—I'll find the money, I'm calling Pamela and rescheduling my appointment. By now I had a terrible pain in my arm near my right shoulder. It wasn't the same as before, not the old feeling of someone grabbing me. This was more of a nerve pulse that would come and go all weekend. I was even starting to lose my range of motion. The minute I called to reschedule my appointment my mood and my arm felt better. I felt back on track.

"So, I want to see what this is about. Why did I keep bursting into tears, and why am I so blocked from feeling the presence of my Higher Self, which is making me feel like a fraud?"

With NMR we learned I was beginning to experience the feeling of unconditional love and it was overwhelming me. I craved the feeling, I feared the feeling, and I felt unworthy of the feeling.

"But we *did* the worthiness thing and it was okay," I said in frustration.

"Here's what I want to say to you," Pamela explained. "There are many techniques for altering energy—massage, sound, light—all kinds of tools for altering energy, which includes emotional programs because they're a form of energy. But if the level of consciousness that created the energy we're trying to change hasn't altered its *thinking*, it's going to recreate that energy.

"So sometimes we do the reprogramming, or we keep doing it hoping it's all been changed, and the change is permanent. When it isn't, that is a strong indication there's still an inner level—it could be an inner child, a teenager, something in this life, or something in a past life—still feeding into 'I'm not worthy.'

"And to put it really simply, it's a call to work with yet another level that hasn't altered *its* thinking. We like to think that when we work with, say, the three-year-old, it changes the seven-year-old's thinking. But more often than not that isn't true.

"Sometimes there are things that happen at three, for example, that didn't happen at any other ages. Sexual abuse is a good example because—and I haven't found any exceptions yet—every age that was sexually abused has to be worked with. A lot of people think that working with one age is enough. But it isn't. Each age has to feel empowered. Each age has to get that lesson for herself. And the work is about helping them come to terms with themselves, understand their life lesson, and feel worthy of moving into that light. What happens to them there I don't know—we'll have to ask the Higher Self sometime. But let's continue with this."

Further NMR revealed my feeling of unworthiness came from a thirteenth-century life as a soldier for the king of France who believed he had committed brutal, evil acts.

"In my experience," Pamela explained, "souls often experience an evil life. It is very important to understand evil. If you don't understand evil, how are you going to combat evil? Every human being has that potential. So if you want to understand that potential you need to experience it.

"What leads to this? What causes people to revert to even less than an animal nature, more bestial than the beast? So we have to help your subconscious grasp this and move into 'I *am* worthy.' Self-forgiveness is what we're talking about here."

And so we were off to my evil life in thirteenth-century France.

"... And now in the thirteenth century, I call for the personality of the soldier from the thirteenth century to shift forward with his thinking, you find yourself moving into that level of consciousness, becoming the soldier personality again with the thoughts that you hold, and the feelings that you feel—a soldier, a soldier in the 1200s."

"Soldier, you have a king you serve. Is that correct?"
"Yes."
"Your king, do you call him by any name or title?"
"To the troops we call him the king."
"And you're a member of the troops?"
"I am an officer."
"You are? So you command others beneath you."
"Many."
"Is there one who commands you?"
"The king."
"Okay. So you command many. Where do you live? Are you always out on the field?"
"Always."
"Have you a family?"
"No."
"So you've been a soldier...."
"All my life."
"Even as a boy?"
"Yes. We all start early."
"And did you become an officer through birth or by earning it?"
"I earned it. I was not moneyed."
"What did you have to do to earn such a position?"
"Be fierce, be loyal, be a leader."
"To your king. What kind of king would you call him? Is he a good king? Is he a fierce king?"
"He's a fierce king. We are not doing this to protect our country. We are doing this to expand our country."
"Do you ever think about that?"
"Yes. We want to expand our country."
"To make your country safer?"
"Well, yes. To fortify."
"And in the name of expanding and fortifying the country, what kind of things do you do when you subdue?"

"Everything. If we need to destroy, we destroy. If we need to kill, we kill. We do whatever we need to do both to save our troops, save our men, and to follow the king's direction to secure and expand borders."

"Do you ever feel uncomfortable with this?"

"Only when I lose someone close that I knew. I have to detach from the foot troops who are killed in large numbers. Otherwise I couldn't do this. But it is personal when it's someone that I knew, a friend or comrade or equal."

"Do you ever feel for the people that you must remove, kill?"

"The children. Sometimes if we have to overtake a hamlet, it bothers me that we have to destroy whole communities and people. But especially the children, the women and children especially. But I have to do it. That's just something I have to do."

"Did you have to learn this detachment? Did you have it as a boy or did you have to gradually...."

"No, you just have to have it. When you're a boy in the foot troops, you almost have to detach yourself from yourself, too, because you know there's a 90 percent chance that you're not going to live. So you just detach. To get rid of the fear."

"I see. It must serve you very well."

"Oh, absolutely. It's a necessity."

"Indeed. That presents a problem for us. I wish you to go to your own death so we can solve this problem. Move forward now and be there just prior to your death and tell me where you are."

"I'm in a tent. I've been wounded with an arrow that is barbed so when it enters the body you can't pull it out. It's right there." [He points to his right shoulder where my pain is today.]

"So it's there in your right shoulder. What are they doing about it?"

"They dug it out, but it's infected, and I have a fever and am delirious and shaking. If it hadn't gotten infected I would have been fine. I probably wouldn't have been able to use my arm much, but I could have lived. But it got infected and I'm dying of infection."

"Do you know that you are dying?"

"I'm delirious. I knew right before I went into the delirium that this was probably it."

"How do you feel about that? Any feelings?"

"I died in battle. I died doing my job, defending my king, defending my country. It's an honorable death."

"Go to your moment of death when you actually leave the body. Be there now and tell me what you are observing and thinking as you leave the body."

"As I leave the body and I leave the tent I see fields and fields of dead bodies and I know that I am responsible for them. And it comes to me what I've done throughout my life. There are massive, massive numbers of dead bodies. Dead bodies everywhere. I think, 'Oh my God, what have I *done*?'"

"What happens now?"

"For a long time I'm just *there* and I start to cry. And I realize how misdirected I was to do that. And all those people, all those bodies, have experienced what I'm experiencing leaving their body. But they don't have to look at thousands of people that they're responsible for. They've just left families and loved ones. I've left fields and fields of dead people.

"I have to do what I can do to stop this. I have to get to the king. I have to make the king understand it's not worth it. He doesn't see these bodies. He sits there in his furs and doesn't see these bodies. He comes out to visit when there are no battles going on. Very good timing! I've got to get to him. I've got to make him understand."

"How do you do this?"

"I don't know. I know I'm different now. I know I don't have a physical presence. But there's got to be a way. I can talk to his mind. I used to have dreams. Maybe I can use that. Maybe I can talk to him that way. But that's what I've got to do. I've got to go to him."

"And do you?"

"Yes. I go to the castle. I'm there now. And he won't—I can't get to him."

"And what do you do?"

"I talk to his mind and I pull at him, I tug at him, but he won't listen. I talk to him in his dreams, but when he wakes up he doesn't remember his dreams. He doesn't want to know. He doesn't want to hear this. He's all about power.

"I thought he was a good king. I thought his intent was honorable. But he won't hear me. He won't hear anyone who is telling him to stop. There are many people telling him to stop. And he won't do it. So I've changed my mind. Oh, this is terrible. All this time I thought I was serving a good king. Now I just keep seeing all those bodies. I'm doomed. I think I'm doomed to this vision."

"And is this where you remain, doomed in the vision?"

"Yes. I'm still struggling to get to him, but it's not happening."

"Would you be open to counsel?"

"Oh yes. This is terrible. I don't want to continue with this. But I don't know what else to do."

"Then I ask you, commander of many, to close your eyes and when you open them again you will *not* see the field of dead soldiers and the field of dead bodies. You will see a light. Tell me if this happens for you at three, two, and one."

"Yes."

"That light has counsel for you. But you must move into it to receive that counsel. Tell me if you are fearful in any way."

"No. It's glorious."

"Good. How does it feel?"

"Oh, it's wonderful. I feel surrounded by it."

"Then as you move into that light, what happens?"

"I feel free."

"You feel free of the doom?"

"Yes."

"And you feel free of the vision?"

"The vision, the doom, the guilt, everything."

"Then in that feeling and that light, ask to have understanding of the lifetime you have just left. And as you ask that, tell me what happens."

"I'm being told that I had to live that life and commit those deeds to see the error of it and to see the error of aggression and the cost of personal gain and ego gain, and I had to commit those deeds and be part of that aggression to fully understand evil. It's almost like I had to be evil to understand evil. And I followed blindly. I did not question the true intent."

"And now?"

"It is necessary to be aware fully of the true intent of a cause when you give yourself to that cause."

"A very valuable lesson, would you not say?"

"Yes."

"Would you, then, call this a very valuable lifetime?"

"Yes. It is unfortunate, all the dead bodies, but I can see now where that was going to happen with or without me. I was involved in it for a reason. It had a purpose, and now I will carry that understanding with me wherever I go next."

"Excellent. Ask that light where you are if it is necessary or important to heal the soldier's shoulder of its infection so it will not bring it back into another life. Would that be important?"

"No. The infection was simply there because it was time for me to end my life lesson."

"Very good. Thank you. And now that you are there in that unconditional love, you are comfortable, you are at ease?"

"Oh, yes!"

"Then you have earned that place. And as you remain there I come now to speaking to this subconscious mind at the level of the body of Ann in the twenty-first century. There was a time, a past life, in which great understanding of self-responsibility, of compassion, and of the importance of knowing the true intent of a cause was lived, an important lifetime in which the lessons and the understanding of evil were understood—a very valuable life lesson, a very valuable time, a very valuable awareness that has been lived.

"Even within the very light itself this was verified important—sent to learn those experiences, successfully completed, successfully reached, the understanding and mastery that flowed from those experiences. Done well. Well done. You can, indeed, feel good about your spirit, good about the choices that you have made, and good about the realizations that have come from them. Life and death and all that comes in between are all simply part of the experiences of spirit. All have validity. All have value. And when the individual spirit that has been a part of it comes to a full understanding, not only does all of spirit gain but that individual spirit gains as well.

"And so we remove from the thinking: 'I am evil.' Evil is merely a thought form created to bring forth messages, awareness, and understanding. So removing now that thought: 'I am evil, I am bad, I am not worthy,' erasing that as you think of the glory of your spirit, as you think of the experiences here on this Earth plane you have had and grown from and gained from.

"Putting now energy here into that shoulder, you say to the cell memory of the shoulder, 'The arrow is gone. It was another time, another place. The infection now, in this light of understanding, has been healed. You will never again be injured in that manner. You are protected because the lesson is understood, which means all nerve damage can now be repaired very rapidly and the arm can now become again whole and healthy and comfortable. Such a powerful, important understanding.

"And as you move now into that desire to be in full conscious awareness, hypnosis is over at one...."

"That was really something!" I exclaimed. "This poor arm has really taken a beating! My little girls used it, and my Dutch guy used it. Now my soldier used it. And the pain always relates to the event. This was a good regression. I felt like I was really *in* that soldier. I kept seeing that field. And you know, I've *never* been able to look at pictures of Civil War battlefields with all those bodies. Isn't that something?"

"Really?" Pamela replied. "So it sounds like that part of your spirit has been stuck in that vision and time and place up until now. He even said it himself, 'I'm doomed to this vision.' But we altered that so he could get his understanding, and you have taken back another piece of your spirit, in a sense."

"And a big chunk of worthiness," I said with relief.

"Yes. And with the arm probably your subconscious kept saying, 'There's something important, there's something important.'"

The NMR we did at the end of the session confirmed that part of my spirit was now feeling worthy and I was feeling worthy of unconditional love and my Higher Self connection.

"You know, Ann, sometimes when you do feel that unconditional love there's a lot of weeping. But now you're going to notice that the feeling is different, not as frustrated. This was a *very* important regression."

This regression allowed me to deepen my experience of the unconditional love of my spirit, my Higher Self. It made me feel invincible. It made me feel powerful. And it made me want to help others feel the same. I also gained a much better understanding of the purpose of evil and suffering—how they can be part of a soul's plan. Now when I witness evil and suffering, rather than getting angry, I start looking for the lesson.

Chapter 18

HOW TO AVOID KARMA FROM AN EVIL LIFE

My evil soldier had learned his life lesson and moved on into the light—or so I thought. This regression demonstrates the vital importance of allowing a distressed personality to speak for itself and come to its own emotional realizations.

The pinched nerve feeling in my arm had returned, and my arm was itching like crazy again. Through NMR testing, we learned the origin of the itching was frustration in this life. I was frustrated about my life purpose. In an earlier session, I had learned from my Higher Self that my life purpose is to teach what I learn in this therapy process. I had been transcribing my tapes and keeping notes to support this, but I did not feel worthy to teach. This unworthiness was coming from my soldier life. My soldier was still present.

"What does *that* mean?" I asked.

"It means he has not stayed in the light."

"So it means he is still present with me?"

"Present in your thinking," Pamela answered. "It's like an inner child who is still present because it is still unsettled. Well, he is still present. He didn't do a lot of talking, a lot of dialogue. We sort of did some *convincing*, and he had his experience. Now we need to find out what he's thinking and feeling. So let's talk to him, and then I'll talk to your subconscious about worthiness.

"He won't listen to me and he won't listen to you, but I suspect he will listen to the Higher Self you both share. So we're going to have you communicate with that inner part of him, and we're going to have him communicate with that inner part of him.

"What a beautiful demonstration this is! We did the regression and many people would think, 'Okay, it's done' and go away and not come back. But here is a good example. You came to your understanding of it, I came to my understanding of it, but he hasn't yet come to his understanding of it. And although you said, 'It's good, it's fine, it's okay,' and I said, 'It's good, it's fine, it's okay,' past life personalities have to arrive at this awareness for themselves."

"We told my subconscious that what he did was okay, didn't we?" I asked.

"Yes, but that didn't change *his* mind. Let's put it this way: Your subconscious serves your soul. And when I talked to your subconscious and said, 'That was fine, let's alter it, you're worthy, it's good,' your subconscious said, 'Fine, except there's another part of me, another part of the soul, that's telling me: not true. So I can't accept it, I can't embrace it wholeheartedly because I serve the soul and there is a part of the soul that is saying: not true.'"

"So when we asked if I felt worthy now, why did I get a yes?"

"What were you thinking? Do I, Ann, feel worthy? You got a yes. But perhaps if we had said 'my soul' or 'my soldier' feels worthy, we would have gotten a no. Or, at that very moment while he was in the light, of course he felt worthy, your soul was feeling worthy. But now, this time, if he's moved out of that level of consciousness, he's moved back into an unworthy feeling. So again, the NMR is correct for the moment and is correct for the way you word it and what you're thinking.

"You know, when I'm doing a one-time past life for someone, I always say to them: I really would encourage you to return to check and see if this has accomplished everything. If it has, fine, good-bye, you don't owe me anything. If it hasn't, then you're going to have to consider that you're not quite done.

"All right, let's go back to France." After the induction my soldier stepped out and took center stage.

"Hello again, sir."

"Hello."

"We have communicated before."

"Yes, I know."

"You spoke to me of your life."

"Yes."

"You spoke to me of your horror at discovering upon the end of your life that you were working for a cause of which you did not approve."

"I can't believe I was so stupid. I was so righteous and violent, and anything that got in the way of the cause just got massacred to expand the borders for my country, for my king."

"Which was your duty, am I correct?"

"Yes."

"You lived a life of duty, then."

"Yes. And I know I thought I was doing the right thing. That was my purpose in my life. That was everything. I had no family. That was my *life*. And I truly felt it was the right life. I had found my purpose. I had found my destiny. I was honorable. And in order to be honorable, I had to be brutal, I had to be vicious, and I had to be what I see now as evil.

"But it was so horrible when I saw those fields of bodies. And then, I went to the king and he ignored me and I saw what was *really* going on. How could I have been so dumb? How could I have not seen? I can't get rid of this feeling that it was all wrong, it was all a sham. I was being used."

"Have you a church?"

"Well, in the camps we'd have a religious gathering a couple times a month."

"And who would lead them?"

"A monk."

"Did he speak of God?"

"Yes."

"Did he lead you in prayers?"

"Yes."

"Did you ever pray by yourself?"

"No."

"What was your thought, your thinking of God? Did you ever think of that?"

"Well, kind of. I thought there was a God. I figured that what we were doing was so correct, that there was a God watching over us. I didn't pray to God to stay alive. The monk would pray for success in battle. I did that. I went along with that. But my thought before going into battle wasn't to God to help me win this battle. It was more to *myself* to help me win this battle. And I didn't realize then the connection."

"And what do you realize now, after the death of your body?"

"That by asking yourself for victory, you're really asking God for victory because we're all God. God is in us all."

"And if that is true, why have you not remained there with that light that you went to?"

"Because I keep seeing all those dead bodies on that field. And I keep seeing that king, that pompous king, walking around his castle, just demanding more and more and wanting more and more. Now I know what his motives are—pure ego and selfishness and his own reputation in history. He's not thinking about anyone's good but his own. And that just keeps coming back to me. And I keep going back there and trying to get to him."

"Let me see if I have this correct, if I can sum this up. The king does not seem to know what is really right, what the truth is. The monk didn't really seem to know. You didn't really seem to know. So maybe that which makes you think you perhaps *do* know now, maybe you need to stop and pause and think, 'Where *is* the truth? How do I find it?' If everyone around you seems to be mistaken, and if you were mistaken yourself, where does the truth hide? Where does it reside? Where can you go to get a true understanding of the whole scene, of the whole picture, of the whole life, the king's included?"

"Well, now that I'm not in that life anymore, I can see it. So it must be somewhere in other . . . other realms, other consciousnesses. And they were *all* manipulated—like the monk, for example."

"Indeed. And now you yourself are in a mindset. And I ask you, sir, if you have the courage, the same courage you displayed on the battlefield, to become quiet and move within yourself and see what that God within you that you refer to would have to say."

"Yes. It's not really courage. It's more desperation. I don't want to be like this anymore."

"All right. Then become quiet and stop your thoughts about the king. And in order to do that, stop your thoughts about the fields of bodies. And in order to do that, begin thinking of light, pure light, as though all your vision and all your feeling is focused on light. It may begin as a small ball of light, even a pinpoint, but think of light. It may take different shapes and sizes, but think for a moment of light until you are filled with it. And now, what would you ask this light?"

"Why did I allow myself to be used?"

"Now listen for the answer. When you have it, tell me."

"I'm being told it was a lesson that I can learn now if I want to. And that was the purpose of it all."

"And what have you learned? Ask it!"

"To always seek the truth. The truth is within you, and if you follow blindly you won't find your own truth. You need to find your own truth."

"How? How do you find that truth within you? Ask that."

"I'm being told you need to ask. But you need to *know* to ask. And I'm being told not to beat myself up because I didn't know to ask. I'm learning now, and it's never too late. And I can realize the lessons from my life now and move into this beautiful light. I can be in this light always.

"I'm being told now, 'You know your lesson of always seeking your truth. You don't have to think about all those dead bodies. They were all part of a plan, a plan much bigger than even your king. So if you feel like a pawn and you hate your king and you feel manipulated by him, just remember he was part of the plan also. And he was being used, as you call it, as much as you were. He did what he did for a reason. And he wouldn't listen to you for a reason. If he had listened to you, that would have upset the bigger plan.

"And you will find out more about the big plan. It has to do with population control and people learning evil. There are so many aspects to this plan. And you were a key part of the plan, and you did your job well. So relax, enjoy the light. You were part of this plan before you were even born. You did your job well and you should be able to feel the joy of being in the light. So come into the light and have the joy of being in the light.'"

"Sir, have you doubts of what you've heard?" Pamela asked.

"No. I can see it clearly now. And I'd love to know more about planning it all before I was born. But I'll find that out in the light, I'm sure."

"Would you like to find that out now?"

"Absolutely."

"Then close your eyes and think of when you were being told about the plan and were being asked to participate in it. Because now you are a spirit and you travel by your thoughts. So think of being in the moment and the time in spirit when you are making the choice, making the decision to go into the Earth planes, into the lifetime. Move into that very moment now at five, at four, at three becoming aware, at two, at one. Are you alone or are there others with you?"

"There are others with me. They are helping me decide on my lessons for this time around."

"And what are you considering?"

"To experience evil and learn the lessons of living as an evil person. I am also taking on the lesson of finding my truth within. So I need a life that will allow me a career that brings out all the vicious aspects of a personality and follow a leader and then find out that it was all for naught and come to the truth of the master plan.

"So I'm going to be born into the body of a peasant and start my journey towards a success of the wrong kind so that I can realize you have to question. You must question in your inner depths and find out what is your truth and learn the lesson of not doing that. And it's a hard one. But the ultimate goal here is enlightenment, and this one is very important. But I guess I'm ready for it now. So I'll do it now."

"As you look forward," Pamela instructed, "as you look into that unfolding lifetime, look to the end of it, and as you see your spirit now, be there as you leave your body. You see the fields and fields of dead. See their spirits rising from their bodies. See each being that did his or her job in that lifetime, lifting from the body and all moving towards the light. Can you hold that vision?"

"Yes."

"All those shining souls moving towards that light to their true home, to their true place, to where they are, like you, reaching understanding of what their life meant and what their death meant. Let that vision supplant the false one as the bodies return to the soil to feed the earth to allow nature to continue to live and breathe. And, sir, as you again move yourself into that light, joining those other souls as they're moving to the light, do you feel coming from them any hatred?"

"None at all."

"There. You're all part of a grand scheme, a grand plan. And so, as a unit, you move. And all those soldiers and all those town folks, you all move as one into the light. Good.

"And now you too, Ann, feeling that experience, aware of that awareness, you think to yourself of how a soul evolves and grows over many lifetimes, many experiences. And each experience is part of a grand plan. Feeling that connection with your Higher Self, feeling that magnificence of your entire soul, you think to yourself, 'I know I have a purpose in this life. I know I am being guided on my path of purpose. I choose to trust my higher guidance, to know it is leading me truly. And with each step I take, the new knowledge there is revealed. I have faith that all that comes after is part of my purpose, part of my plan, part of the grand plan.

"And as you move back into full conscious focus and full conscious awareness at one...."

Through NMR after the regression, my Higher Self confirmed that the soldier was at peace and all parts of my soul were feeling worthy.

"Now my next life after the soldier was the Boston merchant. And he certainly didn't find his truth. How come?"

"Life lessons don't necessarily happen in sequence. It's the big picture that's important. And think about it. If your Boston man had come in knowing the lessons of the soldier, he wouldn't have been able to learn the lessons he—you, your soul, your spirit—set for *that* life."

"Oh, I get it. Just because you learn something in one life doesn't mean it might not be part of another lesson plan in another life. Does it ever end?"

"Yes, it ends. When your soul has learned all it wants to know and has accomplished all it needs to do, it moves beyond physical embodiment and into higher levels of spirit."

After this regression the signals stopped. No more jabbing, grabbing, throbbing, itching arms. No more bursting into tears. Finally! Of course there will always be new signals, but by now I understood how to find the message of the signal. Most of the signals these days are telling me to acknowledge and express an emotion rather than intellectualize it away. What I have learned so far through this work has changed how I see everything in my life, in other people's lives, and in the world at large. The more I learn, the more everything makes sense.

REFLECTIONS

*I*n addition to the inner ages I've written about in this book, other ages from this life also signaled me for help. They all had one thing in common: they needed to express their feelings and understand the experiences causing their distress so they could alter the thoughts created by that experience. In regression, I went to the adoption nursery three times to help my newborn with her fear, her anger, and her feelings of rejection. My three-year-old and five-year-old came forward several times. They too felt fear, hurt, rejection, and deep unworthiness. Each of them showed me how important these ages are in childhood development. While inner ages continue to surface from time to time, I've learned to help them with their concerns myself. In the years since I did this work, no other past lives have signaled me.

During the course of my work with Pamela she shared many stories of her work with other clients. Some healed physical disabilities, including asthma, diabetes, heart disease, chronic pain, depression, cancer, the autoimmune diseases, bi-polar disorder, autism and ADD, addictions, erectile dysfunction, infertility, and weight. Even a brain tumor disappeared. Then there were stories of healing emotional dysfunctions, including depression, suppressed anger, and so many forms of feeling unworthy—unworthy of joy, of love, of respect and acknowledgment, of being attractive, of prosperity and accomplishment. I liked the children's stories the best, like the little girl who used her mind to go for a ride in a red convertible to throw her cancer cells in the ditch.

There were also many stories of spirit attachments wreaking havoc with people's bodies. Sleep walking, tremor diseases, Tourette's syndrome, unexplainable rage, schizophrenia, multiple personalities, violence, abuse—these things and more can be caused by the thoughts, beliefs, and emotions of spirit attachments interfering with a person's brain and body chemistry, thoughts, and emotions.

I had some experiences with spirit attachments, but their interference with my body was less dramatic than others I heard about. I might sleep ten hours a night and still be fatigued the next day or I might become irritable or dizzy. I learned to keep spirit attachments away by visualizing myself surrounded with gold light.

Through this regression work, I discovered my soul lessons for this lifetime and also lessons that I had failed to learn in earlier lives. The universal lesson for all my past life personalities as well as the inner ages of this life was finding their spiritual self—their inner light or power. This lesson is common to all souls living the human experience. We can only find truth, peace, and happiness by reconnecting with our Higher Self and listening to our Higher Self's guidance. Learning this truth *before* we die allows us to live our lives in joy. And what an experience that is!

I have two new best friends. One is my Higher Self. I now talk to my Higher Self constantly. I ask it for guidance. I ask it for dream interpretations and for the meanings of signals. Often I'll ask a question before I go to sleep and request that my first thought in the morning be the answer. I always get an answer. I keep a journal of what I ask and what I'm told. I totally trust in the protection of my Higher Self and know it will not allow anything to happen to me that isn't meant to be.

My other new best friend is my body. I also talk to my body many times a day. I thank it for staying young and healthy. I praise it and acknowledge it as part of my team along with mind and spirit. And because it feels appreciated it complies when I ask it to do something. I've lifted my eyelids and straightened my teeth. I've restored the elastin and collagen in my skin. I've grown in a toenail and rotated a toe. I've healed a sprained wrist overnight. We've fought off the flu together. I keep it alkaline with positive food and positive thoughts so cancer and other undesirable cells cannot grow. I also pay attention to the signals my body sends me. Usually they mean that something is out of balance, and I'm always amazed at the symbolism. For sample body dialogues see the "How Our Soul Uses Our Body" section of my website at www.signalsfromthesoul.com.

Besides befriending my Higher Self and my body, another valuable result of my journey has been a shift in perspective. I used to think things "just happen." I remember, when I first learned that everything happens for a reason, exclaiming to Pamela, "What? Everything? I have to look for reasons in everything?" She answered: "If you want to be the creator of your life, the answer is yes." I've learned to think of my life as a jigsaw puzzle. Where does this piece fit? Where does that piece fit? This is much better than sitting back in the observer's chair wondering: "Why is this happening to me?"

Once I understood the reasons, everything began to make sense. For example, the metaphysical message of a cold is often confusion. A bout of indigestion was signaling there was something in my life other than food I wasn't digesting.

The vitamin tablet that got stuck in my throat was signaling I wasn't speaking my truth at a job. A back wheel flat tire on the Interstate was a signal I couldn't "go back" to the situation at the destination I was driving toward. (I went anyway and came home after four days, realizing the situation offered me nothing.) A rear end collision that nearly totaled my car was a message that a project I was headed to would hold me back, as well as a message to be aware of all things around me. It was also my first out-of-body experience. I actually looked down on myself in my demolished car.

The emotional programs that had been buried so deep in my subconscious and gave me so much trouble have been resolved and reprogrammed. I feel like I've pulled myself out of emotional quicksand. Although my life lesson of rejection still pops up from time to time, I no longer need to be in control or be perfect. I can trust relationships. I don't need to rescue everyone. I don't feel unworthy—of love or money or anything else. And although I'll have to keep you posted on this one, I now know I can speak my truth in a marriage.

I see every single, solitary thing that happens in my life, and in everyone else's life, from the perspective of the soul's story. It's kind of like watching from a mountaintop. I still participate, I still *feel*, but I am rarely upset by things people do or say because I understand now that everyone is on their own path, working out what they have to work out. It's their deal, not mine, so what's to judge? This perspective changes everything.

Some of us might be a little further along on the path to higher consciousness than others, but that's because of many challenges and a lot of hard work. So how could any of us even entertain the notion that we're better than another of our fellow humans? Money, status, power—in the end they mean nothing. Life is all about consciousness and fulfilling our purpose. Now when I pass people on the street or encounter them in any situation, I see other spirits on their soul odyssey—the same as me.

There are times when something irritates me. But now I ask myself: What am I supposed to be learning here? Spirit is stronger and more powerful than *things*. Pain is a *thing*. Suffering is a *thing*. Loneliness is a *thing*. We can use spirit—we can use what is *alive*, including the spirit within the cells of the body—to master matter so that it is in the same joyful vibration as spirit. The result is joy!

We are meant to live our lives with a core feeling of fulfillment. If you aren't feeling fulfilled, I urge you to make use of the knowledge in this book. Yet everyone is on his or her own timetable. If it's your time to make this information part of your journey, I am happy for you beyond words. If it isn't, no problem. Someday it will be your time. As Pamela explained to my subconscious in one of the sessions:

> Within every soul there is that knowing. But they forget. They turn away. They are fearful to see the suffering. They are fearful to see what they don't want to see. But you know that within them there is the part that is urging them to look, behold, see: "I bring for you something of great importance. Look beyond the obvious. Look deep into what is behind the physical. Look into the metaphysical."
>
> There is more to life and existence than everyday, day-to-day human reality. *Explore* the rest of it. *Explore* the spiritual causes, *explore* the spiritual reasons, *explore* the spiritual reality behind what is happening physically. This is what brings the joy that cannot be taken away. This is what brings the love that cannot be lost.

SAMPLE NEURO-MUSCULAR RESPONSE TESTING

*A*lthough every regression with Pamela began and ended with a Neuro-Muscular Response (NMR) testing session, in the chapters in this book the information received through NMR is only summarized. Yet NMR plays a critical role in the regression process. Thus I am including here additional information about NMR as well as a transcript of an NMR session.

Neuro-Muscular Response (NMR) is a muscle-testing protocol developed by Hugh Harmon, PhD. While applied kinesiology, Psyche-K®™, and other muscle testing techniques are used by many practitioners, these methods are not accurate if a spirit attachment is present during the testing, if precise wording is not used, or if attention is not paid to the thoughts of the one being tested and the one doing the testing. The NMR protocol addresses these issues.

Using NMR before a hypnosis regression offers several advantages. For one thing, NMR can determine whether or not a spirit attachment is present with either the person conducting the regression or the one being regressed. This is vital, as spirit attachments can insert their own memories, thoughts, and emotions into a regression.

The question-answer format of NMR is useful for distinguishing between different kinds of memories. Because the subconscious is the seat of both memory and imagination, a regression can be a mixture of fact and fiction. NMR can separate fact from fiction. NMR can also separate objective memories (a factual account of what happened) from subjective memories (an account of what happened that is distorted through false perception). It is important to know both. NMR can also determine whether a memory—whether conscious or subconscious—is one's own or the memory of another. It can also clarify whether it is a memory from earlier in this life or from a past life. It is not always possible to know this in the regression itself.

In addition, NMR can identify the inner age or past life where one is "going" in the regression and what one will find there. Knowing before the regression if unhealed trauma will be encountered and the nature of that trauma is especially helpful. It not only prevents conscious or subconscious avoidance of the trauma during the regression; the conscious self is empowered by knowing what to expect, which allows the conscious self to be more relaxed and also helps the traumatized inner self talk about the trauma and then heal it.

NMR can also find negative thoughts, beliefs, emotions, or other drivers of negative behaviors imprinted in the subconscious in the past that are still affecting the present. Similarly, it can identify the immediate causes as well as the origin of a physical condition or mental dysfunction. It is also used to determine whether the trauma has been healed, as well as the cause of resistance to healing if healing has not taken place.

For additional information, see the papers on NMR by Dr. Hugh Harmon and Pamela Chilton available in the

"How Our Soul Uses Our Body" section of my website at www.signalsfromthesoul.com.

In chapters 1 through 18, the NMR testings that were part of those sessions are abbreviated in order to highlight the regressions themselves. However, because NMR is integral to inner self regression therapy, I am including here a transcript of an entire NMR testing session.

The following NMR testing preceded my first regression, when Pamela and I were looking for the origin of my bad eyesight (see chapter 2 for that regression). We began, as we would do each session, by testing my "yes" and "no" muscle responses and then checking for spirit attachments. In my first few sessions, Pamela helped me decide what statements to make before testing them. As I did more sessions, I became practiced at knowing what to say myself. The sentences in quotation marks are my statements. "Yes" and "no" in italics indicate the muscle response.

"I want to have perfect eyesight." *Yes.*
"My eyesight is sometimes blurry." *Yes.*
"This blurriness is caused by dryness in my eyes." *Yes.*
"The dryness is caused by environmental factors." *Yes.*
"The dryness in my eyes has something to do with emotions." *Yes.*
"The origin of the dryness in my eyes is physical." *No.*
"The origin of the dryness in my eyes is an emotion." *Yes.*
"The cause of the dryness in my eyes is physical." *Yes.*
"My Higher Self knows this to be true." *Yes.*

Pamela paused the process here to say: "So the responses indicate the cause of the dryness in the eyes is physical, but the origin is emotional. I want you to be aware of the difference between origin and cause. Let's say someone walks in with a cold and I catch their cold. The *cause* of my cold is the virus I picked up from them. Another *cause* was my immune system was lowered. What caused my immune system to be lowered? Maybe I wasn't getting enough sleep. Another *cause*. Why wasn't I getting enough sleep? Maybe I was worried. Another *cause*. What was I worried about? Let's get to there. And so we find the *emotion* is fear. So the *origin* of my cold is fear, though the causes are lowered immune system, not enough sleep, a cold virus. So we're always looking for what started this chain of events. We find the origin—which can be thought of as the root cause—and address that. In the example of a cold, I find and eliminate the fear, but I still have to make certain I get enough rest and build up my immune system."

"So," I asked, "I'll still have to put the drops in my eyes and take care of my eyes? It's not just like, okay, done deal?"

"Sometimes addressing the origin does take care of it all, sometimes it doesn't. I don't want to say you'll do the past life and nothing will change instantly—because it *could*. It could be that the dryness is gone and the blurriness is gone. People are very individual and different. But I also don't want to give you the impression that if it's not gone it means it didn't work. It just means that you now have some physical things to attend to. So be open and observant to what happens with you. And be very cautious of telling anyone, 'This is what *always* happens' with anything. People are so complex. Not only are our spirits complex, but our minds and bodies are complex. Okay, now to the origin."

We began the NMR testing again.

"The origin of my bad eyesight is in this life." *No.*

"The origin of my bad eyesight is in a past life." *Yes.*

"The origin of my bad eyesight is anger." *No.*

"A contributing cause to my bad eyesight is anger." *Yes.*

"I still have the anger that causes my bad eyesight." *Yes.*

"So," Pamela said as she wrote on her clipboard, "that will need to be addressed, which we may be able to piggyback on the past life regression. That's what I meant by complexity."

We continued with the NMR.

"The anger causing my bad eyesight is from a past life." *No.*

"The anger is from this life." *Yes.*

"My Higher Self knows it is important to work with the origin first." *Yes.*

"It's possible," Pamela explained, "that it would have said, 'No, go to the anger.' But it's saying go to the origin. So now we're looking for the lifetime that is the origin of the bad eyesight."

"The lifetime that is the origin of my bad eyesight was A.D." *Yes.*

"The lifetime was before the tenth century." Yes

"The lifetime was before the fifth century." *Yes.*

"The lifetime was before the second century." *Yes.*

"The lifetime was in the first century." *Yes.*

"The lifetime was in the first half of the first century." *Yes.*

"In that lifetime I lived in Europe." *Yes.*

"I lived in France." *No.*

"I lived in Italy." *No.*

"I lived in Greece." *No.*

"What would Israel be?" I asked. "Would that be part of Europe? I thought that is the Middle East."

"I lived in Israel." My leg moved halfway between a yes and a no response, indicating a 'kind of' or 'partly true' response.

"So let's make a guess here," Pamela said. "Try this."

"In the first century I was aware of a man named Jesus." *Yes.*

"In the first century I lived in the area called Judea." *Yes.*

"So what are your thoughts about Jesus?" Pamela asked me.

"Oh, I was raised Catholic. Need I say more?" I said with a smile.

My next statement was: "In the first century I met Jesus." *Yes.*

"In the first century I knew Jesus personally." *Yes.*

"Do you know who the Essenes are?" Pamela asked me.

"No."

"The Essenes were the tribe that Jesus was born into. The Dead Sea Scrolls are from the Essenes. . . . They were very evolved in learning, sharing, and teaching knowledge. . . ."

"I was an Essene in the first century." *Yes.*

"I was not an Essene in the first century." *No.*

"Just double checking that!" Pamela said.

"I was a male in the first century." *Yes.*

"I was a contemporary of Jesus." *Yes.*

"I was older than Jesus." *Yes.*

"So with the Essenes, the older would teach the younger," Pamela explained.

"I was a teacher of Jesus." *Yes.*

"I knew his family." *Yes.*

"I was related by blood to Jesus's family." *Yes.*

"I was related by marriage to Jesus's family." *No.*

"I was related by blood to Joseph." *Yes.*

"I was a brother of Joseph." *No.*

"I was a cousin of Joseph." *Yes.*

"Which would make Jesus a second cousin, I guess," Pamela commented.

"Jesus was a cousin of mine." *Yes.*

"There is something more we need to know before doing this regression." *Yes.*

"My bad eyesight began in that lifetime." *Yes.*

"My eyesight was bad in that lifetime." *No.*

"The blurriness began because of a physical event." *No.*
"The blurriness began because of emotions." *No.*
"The blurriness began because of thoughts." *Yes.*
"The blurriness began because of beliefs." *Kind of.*
"The blurriness began because of disbeliefs." *Yes.*
"I couldn't believe my eyes." *Yes.*
"I was unwilling to believe things that I saw." *Yes.*
"I didn't *want* to see what I saw." *Yes.*

Pamela paused again to say: "Here's a question, Ann. Did you not want to see what you saw because it disturbed you or upset you or made you angry or afraid, or was it because it was against your knowledge, your teaching?"

"I did not want to see what I saw because it made me distressed." *Yes.*
"I saw tragedy." *Yes.*
"I was angered by what I saw." *Yes.*
"I cursed what I saw." *Yes.*
"What I didn't want to see was the crucifixion of Jesus." *No.*
"I was at the crucifixion of Jesus." *Yes.*
"The crucifixion of Jesus made me angry." *Yes.*
"What followed made me angry." *Yes.*
"What happened to the Essenes made me angry." *Yes.*
"The origin of my bad vision began at the crucifixion of Jesus." *Yes.*
"It began before the crucifixion." *Yes.*

"Do you know why I did that?" Pamela asked. "Because while we got a yes, there was the slightest give in the muscle response. So it may have been—and I would take this to mean, and we'll test it—that he saw what was coming. He could see how things were unfolding and what was coming. So he didn't want to see what was coming."

"I didn't want to see what was unfolding." *Yes.*
"My death was traumatic to me in that life." *No.*

"There is something more we need to know before we do the regression." *No.*
"The best place to begin is prior to the crucifixion." *Yes.*
"The best place to begin is when I was a boy." *No.*
"My subconscious already knows where to begin." *Yes.*

SAMPLE HYPNOSIS INDUCTIONS

*I*n the interest of not extending the length of this book the hypnosis inductions that preceded the eighteen regressions have been abbreviated. However, they are much too beautiful to omit altogether. The transcripts of two inductions—one to a past life and the other to an inner age in this life—are reproduced here as samples.

Sample Induction to a Past Life

This induction was to my life as an Essene in the first century CE. For the regression that followed this induction, see chapter 2. Before we began, Pamela cued up a tape of nature sounds.

"So as you relax in the chair," began Pamela, using her hypnosis voice, so soothing and calming, so soft and gentle, breathy—like a mother urging her baby to sleep, *"relax* the jaws, *relax* the neck, *relax* the shoulders. That's it. You're *here* in the room. You can allow *all* the rest of the world, everything else, to be pushed away for this moment in time. In this moment in time there are no worries or cares. The doors are closed. We won't be interrupted by the phone or the computer or by people. You're relaxing in the chair. The sound of my voice is very soothing. The sound of the birds is very soothing. Sometimes you might hear the sound of the tape recorder. All the sounds are familiar. *All* the sounds are comfortable.

"You begin to feel how comfortable it is to be in the chair. The chair feels *very* supportive, very, very relaxing. And in the chair you begin to *relax* your body now. You feel the back of the head resting against the chair and relaxing totally and completely. Perhaps you can even feel the flow of blood into the scalp, into the roots of the hair—that gentle pulse of the blood flowing, that life force that is present there at the top of the head and throughout the scalp. That's good," she purred.

"As you're listening to the sound of the birds you might even begin to imagine that you are somewhere out in nature— somewhere in nature that is *so* pleasant, *so* relaxing. You might indicate to me with that 'yes' or 'no' finger, do you like the feeling of sunlight? Yes? Good. Then imagine that you are in a deck chair or on a blanket. You are relaxed in the sunlight. You can feel the warmth of the sun shining on your face. And you feel right in the middle of your forehead, right where that third eye is, a kind of mini sun that begins to glow, to pulsate. As it glows and pulsates, that warmth flows across the forehead, around the temples and the back of the head and over the top and into the eyelids.

"That very gentle, relaxing warmth of that sunlight feels *so* pleasant on the eyelids, *so* pleasant on the forehead, the face. The eyelids relax—such a pleasant feeling for the eyelids to just let go and *relax* as the gentle, clean warmth of that light flows into the eyeballs, into the pupils, and into the lenses, into the muscles, into the nerves, into every part of the eyeballs. Light flows. The essence of your eyes is light. And as you're feeling that warmth of the sun it seems to you there is a very beautiful white light as well—a spiritual light—gathering all around and behind the eyeballs, flowing into the brain and from the brain to the optic nerves and along the optic nerves into the lenses and all parts of the eyeballs. And every single cell, every single molecule and atom in your eyes, absorbs from that light the vibration, the frequency that that cell needs for its perfect form, its perfect function, for the perfect *balance* of the eyes. It flows into the tear ducts and *every* single part of your brain and your body that is involved with the eyes, and the eyesight is receiving this healing light. And it is *so, so* soothing, *so, so* pleasant to just let go and allow it to happen. To just let go and allow that healing to flow.

"And that warmth of that sunlight, as it seeps deep through the skin down, down, down through all the layers of the skin to deep within that *healing* energy of the sun, that *healing* energy of spiritual light, it relaxes the cheeks, relaxes the lips. The upper jaw and the lower jaw relax. The tight muscles, the tendons in the back of the neck and in the throat, they too relax. Your whole body just feels that relaxing feeling in that gentle, gentle warmth of the sun. Down the back of your neck is a *feeling* like warm liquid spreading outward, flowing, melting away tensions, melting away stress. And the neck relaxes. And as the neck relaxes the whole line of the spine *very* gently, *very* steadily is moved into perfect alignment in the neck, in the upper, middle, and lower back.

"And the upper chest, the torso, the back relax. That warm letting-go soothing feeling flows down the arms into the hands. So pleasant, so pleasant as the sounds in the background fade into the background, as you become aware of that rhythm, that flow of the healing energies within you, the warmth of the sun, the healing light, the blood that brings the oxygen and the nutrients down to the fingertips, to the thumbs. Down the line of the spine deep into the pelvis, the hips, into the abdomen, down into the thighs, and the long thigh muscles relax. The knees, the calves relax. Healing energy flowing into bone and to muscle and tendons and ligaments, into joints and nerves.

"The body feels content. The body feels relaxed as that healing energy flows with the blood flow into the heels and into the soles and into the toes of your feet. And the subconscious now uses that healing energy to move the feet into *perfect* alignment and you think of your whole skeletal system. Every bone moves into its perfect place slowly, steadily, gently. Every bone, every joint, every ligament and tendon, every muscle and nerve being moved into its *perfect* placement as the body in its wisdom under the powerful direction of the subconscious mind uses these powerful healing energies and aligns itself—aligns itself for its perfect health, for its perfect balance, for its perfect harmony.

"Every gland and organ moves into its perfect place, every bone moving into its perfect place as the whole skeletal-muscular system balances. With every breath that you take, this continues. It continues as you breathe. It continues in your waking state. It continues in your sleeping state. The muscles and the bones and the ligaments and the tendons and the joints *all* move into that perfect balance for the perfect form of every part of the body.

"Now as I say the number 100, focus on the number as though it were there on a black curtain in your mind, as though the number 100 were to appear. And then as you watch it, it fades into the blackness and disappears. The number 99 now appears. Perhaps very faint, perhaps very vivid. But look at it for a moment, where it would be on that black curtain in your mind. The number 99 now disappears into the blackness. And as we ask for 98, it begins to form and then fades away. Watching the numbers now as the conscious mind fades away with it. And now 97 fading away into the blackness, into that peace and comfort. That's it. Fading away. Now letting go.

"You feel now the awareness of yourself—of your light. As you feel the lightness of your light, of your spirit, you begin to *feel* yourself drifting, drifting back in time. And as you feel yourself drifting back through time, the conscious mind goes into its perfect place of rest, its perfect place and space of rest. Fading away now that conscious mind, becoming the observer, the watcher through time.

"As you now drift through the centuries, past the nineteenth, eighteenth, a hundred years go by. Past the seventeenth century and the sixteenth, through the fifteenth and the fourteenth century, just drifting back, back through that tunnel of time, giving yourself up to it, and allowing it to just draw you back. The twelfth century, the eleventh passes through. Good. Another hundred years, the tenth passes by. Going back so quickly now—the ninth, eighth, seventh, sixth, back through that tunnel of time, fifth, fourth, back through the third, the second, and into the first century.

"Back into that first half of the first century, into the body, into the being that you are in the first century. Back into that first half of the first century, finding the body of the Essene that you are. Shifting *into* that awareness. Becoming aware of yourself there in the time of the first century in the body that you have now in that first century, into the awareness, into the sense of knowing of self in that first century as the Essene. Taking a moment to become aware of your bearings, becoming very aware of your feet. And tell me now, as you hear the sound of your own voice it anchors you more and more firmly into this time and place in the first century as I ask you: Your feet—are your feet covered or bare?"

(Regression continues on page 16.)

Sample Induction to an Inner Age

This induction was to my fetus in this life. (For the regression that followed this induction, see chapter 6.) By the time we did this regression, I had learned to relax my body with the initial deep breaths, and Pamela could focus more on the regression's spiritual purpose. Before we started, Pamela cued up a tape of the sounds of a gentle wind.

Okay. Sit back. Relax. You might think to yourself: 'As my physical eyes grow stronger, as my physical vision gains greater focus, and as my physical ability to see improves daily, my psychic vision is improving, too. I am open and willing to see spiritually. I am willing and open to seeing mentally, the mental realms. Daily, my psychic vision is opening. I see on the screen of my mind visual pictures, images that are symbolic of the communication I am receiving from mind and spirit. And my ability to discern the meaning of the images I see is clear and strong because I am hearing from my Higher Self and it tells me the meaning of my visions. I am growing more comfortable with the thought of having visions as I grow more knowledgeable about the meaning of visions, as I connect more and more with my Higher Self that can tell me the meaning of the visions, of the images, I see psychically.' Good.

"And then with the next deep breath you notice the whole torso of your body is relaxing. The very soothing sounds—the sound of the wind, the sound of my voice—and your body feels safe to relax into those sounds. Your body, your human coming to trust that the goal we have here is to bring to it greater comfort, greater acceptance, greater love, greater ease in the world, that we are seeking to and working towards helping your emotional self, your human, your body to recognize its needs, to recognize its powerful part in your purpose, in your life, and its reasons for being. And we are opening you more and more to that joy, that willingness to live your life in joy, to choose the actions, to choose in your life what brings you joy in the physical level, as well as the emotional, the mental, and the spiritual levels—for all levels of you—recognizing that they are important and we are working to bring them joy.

"And now as you are listening and feeling physically comfortable, the conscious mind would like to go to a comfortable space and place where it can listen and be aware without feeling, without comment, without judgment. Trusting that the 'baby you' has what is needed to help it in this session, which is that Higher Self part of you. And you will watch them work, how marvelously this unfolds. Good.

"Now on the black curtain in your mind, you see the number 100 appear. As you watch it, it fades into the blackness and disappears. The number 99 now appears and then disappears into the blackness. Now 98 begins to form and then fades away. You see 97 as it fades and fades away into the blackness, that peace and comfort. That's it. Fading away. Now letting go.

"As now time begins to drift by, receding now, going back in the mind, back through time. As you move back through time, beginning to feel or imagine the sensation of the body getting younger and younger. And as you move back through your teens now the body, as you move back each year, becoming smaller and smaller. Smaller and smaller. That's it. Moving back through ten, nine, eight, seven, six—moving back to five, the arms shorter, the legs shorter. That's it. The torso growing smaller at four, three, two—a toddler now. The toddler Ann at one. Now the arms and legs even shorter, the body smaller now before one. Smaller yet. That's it. And now the baby with the arms and legs now so small as the baby is unable to walk at this point and getting even smaller, going back to the newborn. And now back within that womb. Back within the womb with the sounds there in the womb, that feeling being in the womb and that closed space, that's it.

"And now going back, the body—the arms, legs—even smaller. You're that little embryo there in the womb, the baby in the womb. I shall call you baby. I shall call you the baby that's there in the womb. Now go to the sad feelings, baby."

(Regression continues on page 57.)

HOW TO FIND A REGRESSION THERAPIST

*T*o heal the originating thought or belief behind a physical or emotional dysfunction through regression therapy requires working with a professional hypnotherapist, or a psychologist or psychotherapist who uses hypnosis to communicate with inner personalities in past lives or earlier in this life. Not all therapists who use hypnosis work this way. Many do not try to identify the originating thought that created the energy that caused the dysfunction. In fact, not all therapists believe it is necessary to address what happened in the past in order to heal trauma. However, as I learned from my hypnosis experiences, if the originating thought or belief is not accessed and changed, the unwanted energies and the symptoms they create will return.

Above all else, it is critical to work with a therapist who believes the inner personalities must speak for themselves. Inner personalities are no different than the conscious personality—in any therapy, the first step is for us to express how we are feeling about the issue at hand. The therapist telling the personalities what they should be feeling or thinking or experiencing simply makes things worse. The personalities need to understand their feelings for themselves.

So how do you find a regression therapist? Ask people you know. You might be surprised to learn who has done a regression. Many reputable professionals are listed in the Yellow Pages under Hypnotherapists, Psychologists, and Psychotherapists.

When you find a regression therapist you are considering working with, ask for a free consultation. Conduct an interview. And remember that *you* are doing the interviewing. Do you feel comfortable? Do you feel safe so your conscious mind can relax and let the inner self communicate? Trust your instincts.

Certification and training certificates should be prominently displayed in the therapist's office, with a minimum of 200 classroom hours for a certified hypnotherapist.

The critical question to ask is: "How will you help me heal my rage [or my cancer, or whatever may be the issue]?" If the therapist starts talking about shifting energy, she probably does not work with the thought behind the energy. What you want to hear her describe is finding the originating thought and going to the level of consciousness—the inner age or the past life—where that thought was formed. The next step is allowing that personality to express his or her feelings and helping that personality understand the situation and change the outcome in an empowering way so the thought that created the emotion is changed. Finally, the therapist helps the client reprogram the subconscious with a new, positive belief. Anything short of these steps may yield results, but they very likely won't last.

If you find a qualified regression therapist who you feel comfortable with but who doesn't work this way, ask if she is willing to consider the methodology by which you want to work. If she says yes, refer her to this book or to Dr. Hugh Harmon and Pamela Chilton's website (www.odysseyofthesoul.org) for further information.

LIGHT THE EARTH

The most important thing I learned from my Higher Self while doing my regression work is that healing ourselves is a moot point unless we also heal our beautiful planet Earth. What we have created we must uncreate. We humans have created a grave imbalance. Nature will not tolerate imbalance. Nor will nature allow humans to destroy it. It will destroy humans before humans destroy it. This has already started—tidal waves, earthquakes, climate change, and the list goes on. Do we want to continue to live here, or do we want to be obliterated?

But we *can* save the Earth. It is *not* too late. Over and over in my regressions I was made aware of the power of my light. We are spirit incarnated in a human body. Our bodies are part of nature. Our spirit self is part of The Light. Light is the energy and consciousness of God (or the Creator, or Source, or whatever term you prefer to use). We are all connected to The Light. Over and over Pamela helped me use my light to feel safe, protected, loved, and guided. Well, it is that light, *our* light, that can save the Earth and correspondingly save us.

Light offers us a simple and deep technique to protect, heal, and yes, enlighten the Earth. As I learned from working with Pamela, thought has power. Ten minds focused on a single thought magnify the power tenfold. One hundred minds magnify the power one hundredfold. One thousand minds focused on a single thought will move a mountain. When hundreds of thousands of minds focus on the single thought of beaming spiritual light to the Earth, Nature is helped to heal the Earth. No words. No prayers. Just light.

The Light of the Creator knows what to do with your light. Offer your light daily. This is not meant to take the place of prayer [or any other personal spiritual practice]. It is a separate offering in which your light joins the Creator's Light for the highest good for the Earth, for you, for your loved ones, and for the world.

Simply focus on the thought of holding the Earth in your hands as the white light of your spirit beams from your third eye to surround and fill the Earth's atmosphere, its surface, the molten magma deep inside the Earth, and the Earth's core with light.

Why white light? It holds all the colors. Why the third eye? It is the center of spiritual thought.

Light the earth daily.

For available resources and additional information
on the topics covered in this book, please visit:
www.signalsfromthesoul.com.

www.ingramcontent.com/pod-product-compliance
Lightning Source LLC
Chambersburg PA
CBHW051752040426
42446CB00007B/324